Too Precious To Be...

A Guide to Restoring Women Suffering in Silence

Tokeitha K. Wilson

This novel is a work of non-fiction. Any references to real people, events, establishments, or locales are intended only to give the non-fiction authenticity. Library of Congress Cataloging-in-Publication Data;

Tokeitha Wilson

Empowerment Station

13 Digit: 978-0-692-57028-9

Dedication

To my MOTHER and Daddy

To the next generation of men and women who will transform the world! GOD put the super on your natural. Selena, you are beautiful.Go forth, follow your dreams, and let the world see your vision through your lens. Messiah, you are an educated, anointed rock star and your love for vacuum cleaners will take you far. Malik, your future is bright. Keep building and create your own world. Sloan, you are a motivator—speak to the world and share your story. Demi, my Goddi, you are gifted. May you flip and twirl into the winner's circle with grace.

Acknowledgements

Thank you GOD for not leaving me in the state and condition I once was in. Thank you GOD for saving ME!

Thank you to everyone and everything, who has ever listened, witnessed, lent a hand, helped to take the edge off, relieved and/or improved me. Thank you to those who have tried to persecute, belittle, hinder, hamper, or obstruct my purpose and destiny. Thank you to those individuals for helping me to understand that every cry, shout, scream, whisper, rumor, or piece of gossip helped shape my future.

Thank you to the Potters who used their power and ability to mold me into the woman I am today. Thank you to my circle of support, personal, professional, and spiritual. Thank you to every Twitter, Facebook, Periscope, and Instagram follower. Thank you, readers, both in print and electronically. Thank you to my family and friends who stand by me despite my highs and lows in life. Thank you to those who believe in me!

I LOVE YOU ALL

Too *Precious* to be…

Hidden
Broke
Molested
Bullied
Abused
Addicted
Embarrassed
Struggling
Captive
Unhealthy
Fatherless
Negative
Ungrateful
Inferior
Disrespected
Deceived

*All opening quotes belong to Tokeitha K. Wilson *

Introduction

When I was a little girl, my mother and father went to prison.

I had moved through a lot of my adult life unaware of how much that had affected me. It was a fact of my life that I just accepted, pushed to the back of my brain and the bottom of my soul, and forgot. I never stopped to think about how being the child of incarcerated parents really shaped my life and impacted the girl I was then and, eventually, the woman I would become. I definitely never thought it would be the catalyst that would launch me into my purpose. But that's exactly what happened to me in early 2015.

I received a call from Mrs. Margaret Quick, Esq., a woman I'd met several times before through my community work and the Department of Human Services. She'd heard me speak at a few events as a representative for my agency. She knew my personal story as I'd shared it transparently with her. After catching up a bit on our personal and professional lives, Mrs. Quick revealed the real reason for her call—to invite me to be the keynote speaker at the upcoming Court Services and Offender Supervision Agency (CSOSA) Women's Conference. The attendees would be primarily female ex-offenders, many of who were mothers.

Yes, I'd spoken in front of an audience before, but this

time would be much different. This was such a significant opportunity for me, not just as a speaker, but as a woman. I'd have to confront feelings and emotions that I'd packed away and a past that held so much pain that I didn't know if I could handle facing it. These women would be coming to hear my soul; to hear something to touch them and to hopefully move their lives in a different direction. I had to find some courage, some strength, some everything—and I didn't know if I had any of it.

As all of these thoughts swirled in my head, I heard a voice that sounded like mine utter the only thing that made sense in that moment.

"Yes."

After confirming the conference details with Mrs. Quick, I hung up the phone. Fear and all, it was time to get to work. I had a speech to deliver soon.

A few days later, I put my son to bed and sat down to get my thoughts out. It was one of the most emotional journeys of my life. As I wrote, my life flashed before my eyes like an action movie's highlight reel—hurt, abuse, pain. I wanted to stop; it was just too much. Yet something kept my fingers moving on that keyboard. And I know now, it was God.

My hand, memory, and heart joined forces together and a powerful story began to take shape. It was as if He had a message not just for the women who would attend that conference, but for me. He reminded me of how much I'd endured and strong I was because of all of it. He reminded me that He'd kept me for this moment. He reminded me that I was too precious, too beautiful, too brilliant to keep my complete story buried anymore. Like an old train carrying too much cargo, He reminded me that I needed to let it all go, for myself and every other woman who was hiding her story, too.

With that invitation to speak, God gave me a new vision, a new reason to press forward, a new reason to speak and to write.

He gave me you.

This book is a glimpse of some of the struggles I've faced in my life, and, ultimately, my decisions to overcome each of them. As I share some of my darkest days with you, I want you to know that this process was far from easy. Trust me when I say there were times that I wanted to conceal, hide, and shove my secrets back inside. I was afraid that people would judge me. I was afraid that no one would ever agree to publish my true story. I was afraid that once my life—and everything and everyone in it—was out there for the world to see, I wouldn't be able to take it back. But I kept writing. I kept telling. I kept pushing past my fear. I stared adversity down. Not because I wanted to. I had to. And you have to do the same.

It is my hope that you will see yourself in these pages, both in my trials and my triumphs. If you are doubting yourself, your worthiness, and your place in this world because of what someone did to you or told you about yourself, I hope that I will share something with you that will begin to erase all of it from your heart and from your spirit. It took me some time—years in fact—to realize that I am too precious to be so many things I'd claimed and believed about myself. So I am here to tell you that you are strong, smart, and beautiful. You are so valuable. You are God's daughter. And if no one has ever told you this, let me be the first.

You are too precious.

Too *Precious* to be...

Hidden

Life doesn't come with a handbook.
Yet it can be a bestseller.

Growing up in Southeast Washington, DC, I attended public school. I was a smart girl, but I had one slight problem—I would always get into trouble for talking in class. In fact, I would get in trouble out of class, too. I just liked to talk. I chatted all of the time, to anyone, and about any topic.

One of my best friends, Michelle, was always shocked at the things I would say out of my mouth. She never knew what to expect when I started to speak. Sometimes she would worry, shake her head, or laugh out loud. I was sassy; my words would repeatedly pierce you like a sword if you crossed me. I was a quick, witty thinker who kept your mind on its toes. I can honestly admit, I didn't always use the power of my tongue for good. I hurt people. But I did the right thing at times, too.

Looking back now, I realize I was forming my pearls.

School was a playground to me, and since I was the only child, every day was a new adventure. I was such a social butterfly. You could always find me talking and meeting new friends. Yet again, my outgoing nature had a downside.

My friends loved me, but my gift of gab was often lost on my teachers. Every year in elementary school, my mother could count on the same report, without fail.

"Tokeitha is smart; she does her work, but she talks too much."

As I got older, my vocabulary grew alongside my boldness. I realized that I could easily engage and captivate an audience. I wasn't shy. I wasn't afraid. I had something to say. So I did. Another pearl.

I graduated from Eastern Senior High School in the spring of 1999, and that fall, I stepped onto the campus at Bennett College in Greensboro, NC. As a freshwoman Biology major, I was so far removed from the DC streets in every sense of the word. I knew from the moment I arrived that something spiritual was going to happen there. I came for an education—I was going to leave with much more.

One afternoon during my first semester, I sat on the front pew of the college's chapel for what seemed like a couple of forevers. Long after our service had ended, I stayed planted in my seat, staring at the stage in front of me. I don't know where it came from, but deep inside, I heard my voice say, "One day I will be on that stage." That became a mantra that I repeated over and over again in my head. The seed of faith was sowed, but I knew this was a big promise. No "average" person could just walk up on that stage to address the women of Bennett College. That was an honor reserved for a chosen few—the academically distinguished or someone who had made a large monetary contribution to the school. But I decided I would be among them and Senior Day would my chance.

My blessing came three years later when my friend,

Monique, was elected Student Government President. With graduation now upon us next year, I knew I had to make my move. While everyone else waited until school started my request to speak was already in writing one year in advance, hours after Monique won President seat. A year later, I stood on stage as the Senior Day speaker of Bennett College's Class of 2003.

It was my first keynote speech and I felt electrified as if I was born to be there. I put my heart into my words, weaving a colorful and compelling story of my best memories, our most significant experiences as a class of incredible young women, and even the lasting legacy of our four college presidents. The student body, alumnae, special guests, and, of course, the Belles of Bennett College jumped to their feet with an ovation when I was done. As I left the stage, Dr. Johnnetta B. Cole, took me in her arms for the warmest embrace. I will never forget that moment. I knew what it felt like to be among a living legend. Dr. Cole is a phenomenal woman and I'm proud to say I am a graduate of her first Bennett College class.

I wanted to leave a lasting impression and make a mark in Bennett's history. I did just that! Not bad for a too talkative little girl from Southeast. God laid all of my pearls out on a velvet cloth that day for the world to see. It was time to leave the campus and new family that I love and see what He had for me next.

I moved back to Washington, DC from North Carolina and soon found myself struggling emotionally and financially, despite the fact that I finished college with a degree, in a science no less. I was a black woman with a degree in Biology (with almost a minor in Chemistry had I decided to take two more classes). Wasn't I supposed to be well-paid, or at least working in the field and a lab that I loved? Wasn't I supposed to be making a mark on this world somehow, researching something, curing something, or discovering something? I knew there was something else for me; I just needed to figure out what it was. In the meantime, I had bills. So I decided I needed a "Good Ol' Government Job." I got interview cute and joined over 1,000 other DC residents in line, hoping for a start in the government with the Department of Human Services. I was number 600.

Have you ever had a moment when you knew God had your back? When you were certain—beyond a shadow of a doubt—that His favor was on you? That was my experience when I walked out of that building. I *knew* that job was mine. I didn't care about the thousands of other people who applied. This was for me. A few days later, the phone rang. It was the human resources department. I got the position. My government career began. And so did my passion for service.

I was a poor girl from a poor family, so my job as a Social Services Representative gave me a chance to see the other faces of government-funded public assistance. I connected to each of my clients personally, knowing what benefits like Medicaid, welfare checks, and food stamps meant to their everyday lives. I found myself going above and beyond; I personally called food banks and community organizations to find extra help and resources. This was so personal to me because even as a salaried employee, at this level, I was one paycheck away from being on the other side of the desk.

I was a natural rights advocate, and God kept putting me in positions where I had to be a leader, stand up for others, and use my voice to help someone else. He thrust me to the front of the room time and time again. I stood in front of managers and public officials speaking on the behalf of government workers and against illegal policies and practices. I served some of the most poverty-stricken residents of the District, acting as their eyes, ears, and voice in the community. With sweaty palms and my heart racing inside of my chest, I accepted the spotlight as the youngest panelist at the Court Services and Offender Supervision Agency (CSOSA) Women's Conference, as the spokesperson for the DC Department of Human Services. The following morning after that event, my Director received an email from one of her colleagues commending me for how well I represented my agency. That was a defining moment for me. With just a few short sentences, Director Brenda Donald elevated my career to the next level. Most importantly, she elevated my opinion of myself. I began to see myself differently.

Won't He do it?

Knowingly and unknowingly, willingly and unwillingly, I use the gift of speech that God has given me. Like the pearl, my gift has been cultivated over the years. My storytelling skills and speaking style were in an incubator, strengthening and growing over time. I didn't even know it, but I was honing my gift, exercising my muscles, and preparing. Even when I felt afraid, I would speak up and out with confidence. I learned how to disagree in a polite, but effective, way. Even when I tried to silence my own voice, people would always point me out and ask my opinion. I could be at church, at my son's school, at work—anywhere and I would be called to the front. I could run, but I couldn't hide.

My voice led me to create Empowerment Station, LLC., and as a motivational speaker and teacher, I want to empower women and their families who are suffering in silence. I am on a quest to show people how to push through pain stemming from low self-esteem, self-confidence, and self-awareness, accept the decisions of their past, and move into a place of healing and peace. My dream is to transform nations around the world and the generations of women before and after me. I want my elders to acknowledge that they are not defeated. Instead, they are victorious. I want the next generation to take every industry by storm with a new wave of innovation and a fresh energy that the world has never seen. I want the youth of this world to believe and dream without inhibitors. I want to join magnificent, globally renowned women like Lisa Nichols and Dr. Cindy Trimm, who have built media empires with their businesses, books, accessories, conferences and galas. I admire both Lisa and Dr. Trimm so much, and I am in awe of what God has done in their lives and in their careers. And you know what? I believe, with everything I have, that if He did it for them, He will do it for me, too. He put this dream in my heart. He has manifested opportunity after opportunity for me to shine. He has picked me up when I fell, comforted me when I cried, and still opened doors when I doubted Him and allowed my fear to overpower my faith. He has even put me in front of Lisa Nichols and Dr. Trimm on social media and both of them have followed, favorited, or retweeted my words on Twitter. Dr. Christopher King told me once to never lose my voice. He told me to always speak up because someone needs to hear my honesty and how I keep it real. *ME.* A little loud-mouthed girl from DC, among giants. The vision that He has given me is profound and so real, I can't help but step into it.

So what does God have for you? What is waiting for you if you were willing to step up and speak up?

Every bad thing that's ever happened to you—every challenge, every moment you spend hiding, afraid, uncertain, and every failure did not defeat you. Those experiences are your marketplace of possibility. It was God who orchestrated it all. When we come through on the other side of an obstacle in life, we reach a higher level. At each level, we get better and better. Each level makes us wiser, and, yes, stronger. Just like that pearl.

Your life is so precious. Do not hide your power within. You are capable of helping someone. Your presence can uplift others. You have the power to enlighten your colleagues. Your energy can be contagious and boost your associates. You have the ability to change any environment. Each one of us has been given a measure of gifts and talents. Some people are geniuses in science. Others are great in math. Some people can play sports and score lots of points. We all have something incredible to give this world. Don't hide it. Don't stifle it in fear. Live the life God has for you.

If you're saying to yourself, "I'm afraid," I ask you, why? What are you afraid of?

____

____

____

____

We all have been afraid of something at one time or another. But that's a part of growing. Life will throw opposition in your face. Obstacles may appear big and problems may seem hard. You may feel overwhelmed. What about the feeling that you're never good enough? It's natural to have all of these feelings (I have them as well). But remember, you were created to survive and withstand any obstacle that compromises your purpose. You're precious and built to last.

Know that fear keeps you in a state of comfort. It is

like a leach, sucking every ounce of potential you have on the inside. The longer you allow fear to be attached to you, the more lifeless you will be. When you are afraid, you're idling and doing absolutely nothing. Before you know it, you have issued yourself a life sentence of going nowhere. Fear will keep you confined mentally, physically, spiritually, and financially.

Fear will show up in your mind, body, soul, and money. Evaluate yourself to see if you've made some of these fear-driven statements like:

I don't want to go to college because it takes too long to finish. (Fear of the Mind)

I only eat one meal a day because I don't want to be fat. (Physical Fear)

I don't go to church because I don't want people in my business. (Spiritually Fearful)

I don't need direct deposit because banks take my money. (Financial Fear)

Remember, if you don't take action then you will stay in the neutral zone—not going forward and not moving backwards. Stuck.

What do you fear? Why does it seem so hard to achieve?

____

____

____

____

Fear can penetrate deep into your body. Yes, even into

your subconscious and subcutaneous layers. Whenever I allowed fear to consume me, I was dead! It was me who allowed fear to hinder my ability. It made me lethargic and weary. Before I realized it, I began to question myself. *Will I be able to? Am I capable of? Can I?*

Am I speaking to you right now?

If I am, know that you don't have to allow fear to win. Start believing in yourself and start saying "Yes!" to you. Instead of "Why me?" change your question to "Why not me?" Encourage yourself, and watch how the more you do, the more that positivity will push that fear right on out. You can rise above your deepest, darkest fears.

Whatever you do, do not hide your gifts and talents from the world. Believe in yourself! Dream Big! Do what it is that puts you on cloud nine! You will know the difference in your gifts. Your gift will never make you depressed. That gift on the inside of you will not make you furious. Nor will your talents irritate you. In fact, your gift is so precious others will wish they had just a touch of what is on the inside of you. You will begin to see the pessimists and skeptics surface and question who and why you are so brave and energetic. The more critics you have, the more powerful your gift has become. Your gift is that BIG, it will drive others crazy. It will inspire applause, but there will be envy, too. (I've warned you, so know you can just block the haters.)

If you are wondering what your gift is, that is okay. My gift was revealed to me through a defining moment, a keynote speaking opportunity. Think back over your life and what God has shown you. Has some unexpected chance to shine come your way or maybe keeps showing up in your life? When your encounter with your gift does happen, it will forever change you. You will no longer think poorly of yourself. You will no longer want to hide or conceal what you have to offer. You will feel like that pearl that was submerged under so much water that when you finally surfaced, it was an aha moment. You may even say, "What was I thinking? What took me so long?"

Come out from underneath and show the world how precious you are. You have something inside of you that will change a generation.

Go invent the next...

Create the latest...

Write the next bestseller…

Design the first…

Start your own…

Orchestrate a billion dollar…

Build a…

You can do or be whatever you dream. It's already on the inside of you. I double dare you to be different!

Write down your gifts and talents. You will be surprised at what you already have.

____

____

____

____

Look at you! You just activated your future. Now, develop a plan to use your gifts and talents to the best of your ability. Chase after your dream every day. Rest and wake with that passion of pursuit on your mind. Be responsible for making yourself happy and going after what you desire. Set goals for yourself every 30 days and get it done. No excuses! It's never too late!

Stop sitting on what God has given you.

You are too precious to hide.

Too *Precious* to be... *Broke*

Every time you think about your dreams, don't hit the brake. Press the gas a little more.

"Shall" is one of the most powerful words on Earth. It appears in the Bible over 10,000 times. If we look at the Ten Commandments, eight out of ten mention the phrases "Thou Shall" or "You Shall," depending on your translation. Throughout American history—from the Constitution to oaths taken for public office to the lyrics of one of the greatest songs ever written, "We Shall Overcome,"— "shall" is right there. If we look at any legally binding document or contract, what word is likely in the terms and conditions? You guessed it—"shall." Such a small word, yet such significance. It is one of those foundational words that command authority. When you see it, you know something important will follow.

When I launched my company, I created a self-improvement program for women focused on personal development and alleviating self-destructive behavior patterns. It is called The Shall Movement. In the program, we go deep and address issues such as:

Overcoming Stigma

Decision Making Power

Bad Habits

Negative Emotions

Non-productive Choices

I'm an expert at all of the above; and I know I am not alone. Think about it—how many times have you given your negative thoughts power, given in to them, and created a self-destructive outcome?

You bought that new furniture or purse, but your mortgage needs to be paid. You hit the party with your girlfriends, stayed out too late, but you had to be at work at 6:00 a.m. You went on a fun-filled vacation, but came home to find your electricity disconnected. These are examples of decisions we make that led, and continue to lead, to self-destructive behavior. It's a snowball effect—one thing leads to another. Before we know it, our lives are chaotic, and we're buried so deep, we don't know what to do next.

But here's what's so incredibly powerful. We can always do something differently. We can always make another choice. We can claim what's rightfully ours. We can always speak a new truth over our lives.

We shall overcome.

You have the power to command authority over your finances, just by changing your language. For example, instead of "I will not be broke," say "I shall not be broke," instead. Which one sounds more impactful? The word "shall' is like a gear of an engine. It forces movement and when you need a shift, you can always use it. "Shall" is so profound, it can change your current condition or state of mind. Think about when you go to church and the pastor says, "Turn to your neighbor, and say "I shall something or other." As soon as you finish repeating the phrase you feel different. You act different. Your mind starts to see possibilities that weren't there before.

I'm urging you to do this when it comes to your bank account. You could be sitting on a financial goldmine. Multi-million dollar enterprises are stuck inside of you. Free them up! Stop holding your talent hostage. Do you know that your gift can create multiple streams of income?

If you were given a lump sum of money what would you do with it?

____

____

____

____

Let me tell you another story.

Growing up, I loved my baby dolls. Baby Alive, Barbie, the super-tall-no-name-brand-ones-in-overalls—any doll I could get my hands on made me happy. But my absolute favorites were Cabbage Patch dolls. I always wanted a Cabbage Patch Pretty Crimp and Curl. Those were the most expensive since they had "real" hair and not that yarn stuff. My mother couldn't afford the doll, so she gave me what she could. A Cabbage Patch preemie. She had hair so I didn't care. I just wanted to make her beautiful.

There wasn't a day that passed that you wouldn't find me braiding my dolls hair. I always used my mother's good hair products and even tried to curl my doll's hair. Of course,

I burned it (not to mention it was full of grease). But here's the thing. I was never formally trained. I had a natural talent for hair.

Once I stopped playing with dolls, I started braiding my own hair. In college, I was known for my braiding skills. And people paid me either with cash or I bartered for the things I needed, like rides to and from campus. My talent was timeless; it was a source of income that always sustained me whenever I needed it to. It never went away nor did I forget how to use it. In fact, it's sought after. People rely heavily on great hair stylists. A braider is like an attending physician when it's time for surgery; it can be catastrophe if you're not present and accounted for.

You could say my gift for braiding is in my genes. I come from a lineage of stylists and barbers. But we all have something God-gifted and genetic in us that can sustain us if we use it. If I lost everything today, including my job, I could braid hair to make money. Just think, my talent was given to me for free. It does not cost anything to use and it can provide for me.

It's precious.

Have you considered becoming an entrepreneur? _________ Why not?

____

____

____

____

You made a list of your talents and gifts in the last chapter, but let's expand on that a bit so you can get a clearer picture of how valuable you are. In the space below, list your talents again and the business or industry each is related to. Be creative.

Talents

Business or Industry

____

____

____

____

____

____

____

____

With one talent alone you shall never be broke. Use all of them and watch your wealth multiply.

Let's take an even closer look. How much do you think you can earn just by using your talents? Write in a level of income for each talent:

Talent	Income

Let me be the first to tell you how valuable you are. There are people in the world that wish they could do what you do. Now that you know what you're capable of, I challenge you to put your talents to use.

Right now, I can start my own braiding salon, or I can become employed at a local braiding salon if I needed a secondary source of income. If you are an artist, you can draw, paint, and design images in movies, paintings, and on clothing. You can design a website or a logo, create a book cover, draw a model, or design a blueprint. An artist can draw cartoons for the local newspaper, or sketch a famous character for an animated film. These are just a few examples of how your talent can create a source of income. Therefore, an artist shall never be broke.

If you are not knowledgeable about your industry or a business you're thinking about starting, do some research. Look for free classes and workshops. Take the necessary steps to get the right credentials, even if that means you have to get a license or certification. Don't worry about what people will say about you when you step out and start your own business or create a new industry.

You **shall** not allow anyone's negative opinions deter you from your destiny.
Your talent **shall** not lay dormant.
You **shall** tap into every new innovative thought and idea.
You **shall** have multiple streams of income.

You are too precious to be broke.

Too *Precious* to be...

Molested

Beware of people in your life who exploit you.

Elephants are some of my favorite animals. Everything about them is just majestic—they can live to be 70 years old, weigh up to 15,000 pounds, and walk for miles and miles at a time. We often see elephants together as a family, the females are true matriarchs and hold everyone together like glue. Like humans, elephants are also deeply emotional. They cry and can suffer from stress and depression.

I recently learned of a tragic story about Raju, an adult elephant that was allegedly lured away from his family as a calf, captured, and held in captivity. For 50 years, Raju was chained and beaten by his owner on a daily basis until he was eventually rescued by wildlife conservationists. When he was found, Raju was severely bruised by his chains and shackles. The story goes that after his chains were removed, he cried. The elephant's display of emotion was so surreal, it deeply moved the conservationists and gave them hope.

As optimistic as the story is, there is still something sad about it. Raju's feet were free and would eventually heal, but his spirit and his heart would be bound and bruised forever. That abuse he endured, every lash, every beating, every harsh word, was scorched on his soul. He couldn't and wouldn't forget.

Children who are molested carry that wound with them for a lifetime. Their youth and innocence shattered, they are vulnerable to everything and everyone. At a time in life when a child is absorbing everything they see, hear, touch, taste, and smell, they experience something that hurts them. And that something and someone never goes away—even after that child is grown, rescued, and freed.

I was seven, almost eight, years old when it happened. I would play with two teenaged girls who lived in my neighborhood. They were cool to hang around and were like the sisters I never had. We used to jump double-dutch and skate together. They were my friends so I thought. Being young and unaware, I trusted them. But that all changed one summer evening.

Under the guise of the game "Simon Says," I was forced to repeat whatever each of them did to me. When "Simon" put her hand between my legs, I had to do the same to her. What began as a touch progressed to other sexual acts. Hands massaging me became fingers inside of me. Fingers soon led to a tongue. At seven years old, I had a threesome before I learned to ride a bike.

Being molested by two girls forced me to deal with my sexuality in a whole new way. I had to accept that my first feeling of pleasure came from the same sex. It was a female hand first placed on the inside of my womb. Then it was a female tongue inserted inside of me. My tongue and hands were inside of another girl. I was just a girl myself.

The abuse had a routine. It would happen when we

would play outside or I would go over to their house. Ashamed, afraid, and confused, I didn't tell anyone. I never thought that someone would believe me. Besides, they told me not to tell. What I experienced was simple: control and intimidation. I was scared silent. I never told a soul. Until now.

When you are violated as a girl or a woman, there is a missing piece of you that dies. You have to accept what was done and move on. I lived with the pain, the self-pity, and doubt, and, like so many other victims, I kept what happened to myself.

Who would believe me anyway?

We see this played out in the media far too often, right? When a woman steps forward with an accusation of rape or abuse, the first response is, "Why would she wait so long to come out and tell?" Let the judgement games begin.

Bloggers write columns based on too much fiction and not enough facts. Radio hosts open up their phone lines for public discussion. News stations find people to interview and old photos surface out of thin air (let's not forget sex tapes). It took every ounce of the victim's strength and courage to be able to accept what happened to them, let alone speak openly about the experience. But she is humiliated, dehumanized and attacked all over again.

So we stay silent.

We want the memories to go away, but they don't. You can try to forget it, and you may even be able to suppress it for years. Then a flashback comes out of nowhere. You touch something, smell something, hear, taste, see something, or visit a certain place that reminds you of molestation. And it starts all over again. They'll always be a trigger; for me it's seeing someone from my childhood or if someone touches me in a playful way or tries to be "funny" with me and act silly, it bothers me. My abuse was disguised as play and fun, so I still have a hard time processing that type of behavior. Like Raju, it's etched on my soul.

I didn't fully face my childhood sexual abuse until I was an adult. I was dating a guy at the time, and he noticed I would get angry and tense whenever he tried to wrestle or play with me in a joking way. When we slept together, I would want him to touch me a certain way. I wouldn't allow him to experiment with me or explore my body the way he wanted to; I knew what made me feel good. Subconsciously, I was replicating my abusive experiences because that's what I associated with pleasure.

"Have you ever been molested?" He asked the question and it shocked me. I didn't think I acted strangely or gave anyone a reason to think that. I totally blew him off and said no. I lied! He was the only person in years ever to pick up on it.

Anyone who has ever been abused as a child finds a way to cope with what happened to them. We all cope in different ways. Some turn to drugs, alcohol, or food. My mechanism was men. I loved men, whether they were good for me or not. I had an infatuation with toxic relationships. I didn't want to be alone and men soothed me. I felt protected, and unlike women, I felt a man wouldn't violate me. I wanted to be loved so badly, so when a man treated me bad, I stayed. I wanted a family and security, so when a man was unfaithful, I was right there waiting when he returned. I didn't care what a man did or said as long as I could say I had one.

I struggled with letting go of a man. A man gave me the feeling of protection and security. I felt safe when a man was around me because it was a female who violated me. I did everything to make a man stay with me despite how bad he treated me. Another way for me to cope was that I wanted a family because I grew up in a single parent household as the only child. I was always attracted to families because I felt a sense of security. The image of a family made me feel protected and loved. As a result, I stayed in toxic relationships because I never wanted to be alone.

Letting go was one of the hardest struggles in my life.

Were you abused as a child? If so, by whom: relative, family friend, or someone else?

____

____

____

____

How do you cope with the molestation?

____

____

____

____

How has the molestation affected you into your adulthood?

____

____

____

____

Like Raju the elephant, I was saved. I endured the pain of being misused, but that wasn't the end of me. I made it through the pain and haunting memories. I am a survivor! I went to therapy and talked through my pain. I found comfort in going to church, knowing that I was forgiven and that I had to forgive as well. God restored me and gave me the peace to accept the things I could not change. He helped me to trust again.

Do you have issues with trust as a result of the molestation?

____

____

____

____

Have you forgiven those who abused you? If you haven't, why not? How long will it take?

____

____

____

____

Have you forgiven yourself? Why or why not?

____

____

____

____

It was so tough for me to forgive. I had to forgive myself and those who hurt me, both intentionally and unintentionally. God had forgiven me and those who had hurt me, so I had to choose to do the same. The anger and pain I carried in my heart and spirit would have destroyed me if I hadn't let it go.

There was a time when I hated myself. As a victim, I questioned my worthiness and value, wondering if I would ever be a whole woman—one without insecurities, confusion, or fear— and be able to move past the hurt I'd endured. But I had to get honest with myself and accept me for me. I had to be good with myself, just as I was. I had to realize that everyone makes mistakes, and, too often, we are just innocent bystanders of someone else's pain. We are all human. And God would not forsake me. Like Raju, I knew that one day I would be free. I'm free today from the pain and shame. My faith helped to restore my mind. But it was my hope that helped to repair my heart.

I am granting you permission to set yourself free today.

If you've been abused and you're struggling and asking yourself, "Why me?" I have a question for you.

What makes you different from anyone else?

We will all encounter loss, pain, and hardship in our lifetime. For most of us, we will face tragedy and loss countless times. But we can't run from it. We can't avoid it. We have to face it. Don't die knowing that you could have let it go a long time ago. If you're still angry and fighting yourself every day, there is a reason. You haven't dealt with forgiveness and sought healing for your pain. There is more power in your pain when you forgive. You will gain peace and that is priceless.

Let it GO!

If you or anyone you know is a victim of abuse, contact the National Sexual Assault Hotline 1(800)656-HOPE.

You are too precious to hold on to this forever.

Too *Precious* to be...

Bullied

We all have a journey. But the woman who takes the journey no one else wanted is destined for greatness.

You know something is wrong when you see them flying around in the sky. They fly high and look low searching for their prey. They're often labeled as the "Bad Guys," the squadron that loves to feast on the dead. The smell of decay is like a sweet aroma to them as they swarm around death. Vultures!

Vultures can smell blood in the air, and bullies can sense fear. These wannabe tyrants prey on your feelings, making you feel sad and unwanted. A bully loves to feel superior, so they use force to show superiority. The kids who harassed me used name calling; some bullies get physical and hit, push, and spit. Bullying can also look like:

Social bullying: Excluded from popular groups, clubs, or left out of the "in crowd"

Physical bullying: Hair pulling, fighting

Cyber bullying: Prank calls, rude comments on social media, nude photos, and degrading text messages

Bullies are like vultures that prey on people that are not "normal." Anyone can be a victim of bullying; even as adults we're not exempt. Sad to say, bullying can happen anywhere: school, work, church, camp, or our own homes. Interestingly, most victims don't actually know why they are being targeted.

Bullying can be a scary thing. And like any other type of abuse, it can scar you deeply.

Chunky Fat Girl, Fatty, Baldhead, Bald Dina.

As a little girl, I was teased in school about my weight and hair. I was already curvy, so my shape stood out from the other girls in my class. I wore my hair in a short afro. So I didn't look like everyone else. The vultures swarmed me and called me ugly names. You name it, I heard it. But despite what those kids at school thought of me, I was pretty and I knew it. In fact, I was just as beautiful as my Cabbage Patch doll. So when they would tease me and call me names, I didn't let it bother me. I always had a smart comment to clap back with. I could go back and forth, or "joan" with them all day. You couldn't insult me and I did not have an equally hurtful response ready for you. My voice was my weapon. And I used it regularly.

Little did those kids know, fending them off was easy. I had defended myself against much bigger bullies. Right in my own home.

Bullies often learn their oppressive behavior at home. Bullying can be passed down in families from one generation to the next. Older relatives may feel a sense of superiority over younger relatives. On the outside, a family may look innocent or harmless. But if their walls could talk, the story would be a lot different.

I was the youngest in the family at the time. A teenage relative said everything those mean kids did and more. She verbally attacked me and called me names. She would walk me to school and smack me around all the way there. When I got home, she would slam doors in my face and lock me out of certain rooms in the house. I felt like I was being tortured every day. I still hear some of those hurtful words in my head today.

By the time I was ready to go to school, the kids in my class didn't stand a chance. I could handle them; it was home that I dreaded. In school I was well prepared to defend myself. But when I returned home, the pain would always greet me at the door. I never forgot what my cousin did to me. Still, I was able to forgive. The funny thing is, years later, when I confronted her about it, she didn't remember any of it. Today, we're in a much better place. We are peaceful, we share, and we talk often. The healing took time and it was not done overnight. There are no hard feelings between us. Only love.

Were you bullied by a family member?__________________

How did you defend yourself against the bully?

____

____

____

____

Did you tell anyone about the bullying (parents, siblings, friends, etc.)?

____

____

____

____

Have you forgiven yourself? How long did it take?

____

____

____

____

As the saying goes, "Hurt people, hurt people." I was bullied, so I became a bully. I was so enraged as a child for a number of reasons, but largely because I was being picked on, talked about, made to feel less than. And while I could lash back out verbally, I still felt small and defenseless. I didn't know how to deal with and channel any of my feelings, so I stomped around with an attitude. And when I sensed an opportunity to pounce on someone else who I felt was scared or weaker than me, I seized it. I had no idea how much I'd impacted any of these people until years later.

We were both grown when a family member pulled me aside and shared her deepest secret with me. For years, she had been cutting herself. I was shocked speechless. I knew she was quiet and appeared a little down at times when we'd get together for family dinners and celebrations. But I had no idea she was hurting herself that way. In my mind, I started to prepare the words I would say to comfort her, to come up with a plan to get her the help she needed and to affirm for her that she wasn't alone anymore. I worked in social services, I knew how to help people. I never had a chance to get one word of that script out of my mouth. She wasn't done. She went on to share with me that there was one person who drove her to depression and self-mutilation. And it was me. I was devastated. I had deeply hurt someone I cared about—out of my own pain I caused someone else to suffer. I felt so low. She held a mirror up to me, my character, and my issues. Those who bullied and hurt me never got to see my tears, my pain, my bruised self-esteem. But here I was, face to face with all of my ugliness.

I never wanted to look at it again.

Heartbroken, I had to get to the bottom of my behavior and why this environment of harshness and harassment was so prevalent in my family. The answer was simple. It was learned behavior and had been a horrible cycle among us for years. We were a hurt people that continuously hurt other people.

After plenty of family meetings, therapy, and discussions via text or in person between all of us, I began to see that self-esteem and a lack of feeling loved played a major role in my behavior and theirs, too. I had to accept that I was bullied and admit that I, in turn, bullied someone else. I realized that I never understood how to develop a healthy relationship with my family or anyone for that sake. Although there were times that the bullying was intentional on my part, other times it was unintentional. I apologized for my actions and asked for forgiveness. We all took steps toward healing.

Today, I am more aware and accountable for my actions. My conscious level has increased. I am more responsive and sensitive to other relatives. I no longer carry the hurt of what was done to me or what I did to someone else. My only hope is that they are not hurting any longer from my inflictions. It takes time to heal relationships and we are making improvements. We are getting there, slowly but surely.

As far as the family member I'd hurt most, we've

made our peace with each other and ourselves. I have a tattoo on my left wrist; it's an infinity sign with a heart. She wears the same one on her right wrist, symbolizing the hand she would hold the blade she cut herself with. Our tattoos are a reminder of the promise we made to each other. The symbol is a promise not to cut and remember to love. She promised not to cut herself again, and I promised to always be there for her and love unconditionally. She is my one and only sister and we are 16 years apart. She is the very gifted photographer behind the cover image for this book.

As one who has bullied and been bullied, I learned a valuable lesson in life. There is good in everyone, flaws and all. We've all caused someone pain, whether we intended to or not. Heal your heart and forgive and make peace with those you've hurt when you can. And while you're at it, make peace with yourself.

A Note About Cyberbullying

The Internet has given bullies more access and a louder voice that they've ever had before. We've all seen a viral video of someone, usually a child, being attacked on a school bus by one or a gang of other kids. The post is shared thousands, even millions of times, and sadly, the bully is an overnight social media celebrity. We've become a world that celebrates and promotes violence against innocent people. Every time we watch or like something like this, we play a role.

Be responsible with what you watch and what you share. Someone's life could depend on it.

You're too precious to be bullied.

For more help on bullying checkout www.stopbullying.gov

Too *Precious* to be...

Abused

Never let the trials of life destroy you.

The Fourth of July is a federal holiday in the United States. A lively, patriotic celebration of our country's independence, Americans mark the day with fireworks, barbecues, family reunions, and carnivals. As exciting as all of the fanfare is, July 4th is really about freedom. It was the day that the United States broke free from Great Britain's reign. It was the day America said, "No More." The country was prepared to go to war, to give life, liberty, and the pursuit of happiness— to die— for its freedom. There was no cost too great.

What does your freedom mean to you?

____

____

____

____

____

Are you free to make decisions in your life?

____

____

____

____

Who or what is blocking your freedom?

____

____

____

____

Abuse changes you. And it comes in so many different forms. The black eyes, the bruised cheeks, the busted lips, the broken bones—those are just the obvious wounds. Those scars are often covered up with makeup, so we don't see them. The body can be hidden, costumed, and altered, but what about what lies beneath? What about the scars beyond the surface? Those can't be covered. The emotional, mental, and verbal abuse doesn't show up as bloody or broken. It shows up as no self-worth. It shows up as negative self-esteem. Sometimes, it shows up as love.

When a man abused me, I thought he loved me. But the reality was that he was controlling me.

"Your clothes are different. Who are you trying to impress?"

"You took longer than normal coming home. Where were you?"

"Did you see that I called? "Why didn't you answer your

phone?"

"We haven't had sex in a few days. Are you cheating on me?"

It started with a few questions. Those questions progressed to a tight grip on my arm or a snatch. Then it escalated to violence—hitting, punching, slapping. All abuse starts small and builds. Don't ignore the red flags. Don't fall for the control, the cheating, and the cursing your name wrapped in adoration and affection. It's all disrespect. It's all disappointment. It's all detrimental to your soul, your esteem, your heart.

The truth is I never knew how a man was supposed to treat me. I grew up in a single-parent household with a mom, and I knew who my father was, but we didn't have a true relationship, a bond. My girlhood was void of those memories and moments that a young woman has with her father—where he shares wisdom, where he holds her, hugs her, and affirms her value. That is such a critical time for women, where her daddy demonstrates, in words and in actions, what a man is supposed to be. I didn't have any of that.

So I did what most women do. I searched for my father, the one I wished I had, in men. And they were the wrong ones. I didn't know how precious and priceless I was. I paid such a heavy price. I had never been hit by a man in my life, not even my father. I never saw a women hit by a man in my life. I never witnessed a woman in my family being abused so I never thought it would be me.

I was so happy. The love of my life had asked me to marry him with a proposal that I'd dreamed about, including a sparkling and very expensive four-carat diamond for my finger. I leapt in full-on bride's mode. I began planning my beautiful and amazing wedding day and happily ever after—what I would wear, who would sing, where we would live. I was so caught up in the fantasy that I lost sight of my reality.

He punched me so hard, I wet my pants. It was as if my body was an iceberg stuck in a frozen-solid ocean. I was there, but it felt like I was somewhere far, far away. I couldn't move. Everything around me moved in slow motion. I saw his lips moving, yet I heard nothing. *This didn't just happen,* I thought to myself. It had.

After what felt like hours had passed, I slowly reached up to feel my bruised cheek. A switch flicked and all of my senses ignited all at once. My skin was on fire and my ear burned. I touched the ear, and I winced in pain. My earring was missing. He'd hit me so hard that my earring split and the hook was the only evidence that my earring was ever in my ear. It must have flown out of the window. My eyes caught sight of everything around me. It looked like a Tasmanian devil had ripped through my car. In his burst of rage, my fiancé had destroyed the inside of my car on the passenger side where he sat. The food we'd ordered was mashed into the floor of the car. The actual interior car door was hanging on by a thread—the wiring was exposed and dangling and the screws were loose. I shifted my gaze to him and found him glaring at me, fists clenched, nostrils flared, and tears running down his face. This wasn't over for him.

A piece of my mind must have snapped and went out of the window with my earring. It took everything out of me not to kill him. I could have intentionally pressed on the car's gas pedal and ended both of our lives right there. I thought about how I would drive us home, make love to him, pull my gun from the pillow, pump him full of holes, clean up, change clothes, and come out and lead a search in ditch instead of a search and rescue for his worthless body. Every ugly thought imaginable crossed my mind. I went into survival mode. The only thing that made me stop and choose life (and freedom over a lifetime prison sentence) was I knew I had to live for myself and my child.

My abuser always found a way to make me feel inferior and convince me that his anger and his issues were my fault. I always knew what was coming based on his actions. If he got angry, frustrated, or panicked, I could expect him to turn on me. The change occurred instantly, just like the Incredible Hulk. Verbal threats always followed the physical abuse, making me feel even more low and helpless.

Like most Hulks, he was often remorseful and apologetic after his destruction. I heard, "I'm sorry, it will never happen again," and "Baby, you know I love you. I don't know why I did that," more times than I could count. Then I would be showered with gifts and family members attempting to soothe the situation and convince me to stay with him. And I fell for it each and every time. I believed him when he said he loved me. I believed him when he said he didn't mean to hurt me. I believed him with my whole heart when he said this time would be the last punch he ever threw at me. It never was.

The next time, he threw me down on the bed, climbed on top of me, and gripped my neck with both of his huge hands. As my mouth filled with blood, I choked and cried out to God, "Please GOD save me, don't let me die!" The harder he squeezed, the louder I cried. I believe that at some point, my cries must have reached heaven. I felt a power rise up in me. I somehow unleashed the extraordinary amount of energy it took to get that man off of me. I flipped into full Tina-Turner-in-the-limo-fighting-Ike-for-her-life mode. I punched, hit, and kicked with all of my strength. I was exhausted, but my mind was disconnected from my body. I didn't care how tired I was or how much pain my body was in, I had to get that man off of me before he killed me.

Somehow, he let go. I grabbed my son and ran into the bathroom, holding him tight to me. The bathroom door kicked open and crashed off of the hinges. My son started screaming, "Don't hit Mommy!" Something in my fiancé must have snapped when he heard our child's voice; he stopped and snapped out of it. Both of us looked like we had been in a war zone. I had bruises from the neck down; my fiancé had cuts and slashes from the neck up. That sparkling, very expensive, four-carat diamond ring had carved his flesh.

That was the worst fight of my life, but that fight was for my life! My mind was made up. I wanted to live. I wanted my freedom at any cost. Both my life and my freedom meant that much to me.

I got out.

As a Social Services employee, all of my professional, on-the-job training was put to the test. I found myself on the other side of my government desk. I desperately needed help if I was going to leave this man alive. I returned the engagement ring and all that came with it. My soul cried out and my "American Dream" was scattered. I was too precious to be abused. I was bitter. I was an emotional wreck. The man who I thought I would spend forever with—the man I thought was the perfect guy— turned out to be a Devil on a Pew.

When I left him, I decided I had enough. This act of courage was for my sanity. No longer would I allow him to hold the power. NO more physical assaults. NO more verbal tongue lashings. NO more emotional destruction. None of it was my fault. I had been blaming myself for years, telling myself I should have left. Shouldn't I have seen the signs? Or did I do something to deserve this? NO. There was nothing I could have done to provoke this man or cause him to hit me. I knew all of this, yet I allowed myself to be abused. I chose to tolerate all of this. I chose to stay.

I had to learn a few things. To trust myself. To be alone sometimes. And what love really looked like. I had to learn that love doesn't...

Bite you.

Kick you.

Break your bones.

Choke you.

Scratch you.

Curse you.

Spit on you.

Punch you.

Slam you down.

Talk down to you.

Pull your hair.

Blacken your eyes.

Threaten to kill you.

I also had to learn how precious I was.

Evaluate yourself and be honest with yourself. I know it's hard, but this is what helped me to see how valuable my life is.

Do you deserve to be abused, Yes or No? If you answer yes explain why you deserve to be abused.

____

____

____

____

Ask yourself, "WHY am I allowing this to happen to me? WHY do I feel this way?"

____

____

____

____

Describe how you feel after each attack? For example, "I feel like I am losing my mind."

____

____

____

____

Taking the time to reflect on my situation gave me a chance to see things clearly for the first time. The abuse and disrespect was always there. He was never different. I just didn't want to pay attention or accept him for who he was. There was always a part of me that thought he would never hurt me like this—he wasn't like that. The truth is we were both broken and vulnerable. He was fighting demons from his past, having witnessing abuse as a child. He had just returned home from prison and I was adjusting to him coming home. I wanted to be a supportive woman, to love him and give him everything I needed, so I kept falling for him and giving him chance after chance. Not only did he hit, he cheated. I knew it, but he never admitted there were other women who served time with him. Those women sent him money, nude pictures, and visited him as often as I did.

I could now see how I'd become isolated and distant. My behavior changed. I avoided people and especially conflict at all times. I didn't want to hear anybody who wanted to tell me about my man or my situation. I was constantly defending us and trying to cover up my mess.

But my family and friends knew something was wrong. I had given up. I became suicidal and continuously thought about harming myself to escape the pain I was in. I had even written out my will, called my brother, and told him to take care of my son if something ever happened to me.

One day, while visiting my parents, my mother asked me if I was okay. Have you ever been teetering on the edge of a breaking point and someone asks you that question? It's as if everything was bubbling up inside of you and your soul was just waiting for a chance to rupture. My heart burst right there in her living room. And I did something I couldn't bring myself to do. I asked my mother for help. That was the first time in my life, that I had ever witnessed my mother helpless. She was so angry that she couldn't say anything. She threw her hands up and exhaled. I was her baby girl, her firstborn, and she couldn't save me. It devastated her. When my daddy came into the room, I shared my story with him. As heartbroken as my mother, he just left the room. Our family changed that day. My parents rallied around me and gave me the strength and support I needed to leave that relationship. They helped me to unlock those handcuffs and reenter my life.

How many times have you been offered help?

____

____

____

____

What it is that keeps forcing you to deny the help?

____

____

____

____

Does your abuser have a history? If so what number are you?

____

____

____

____

Have you ever thought you wouldn't live to see the next day, month, or year?

____

____

____

Are you willing to die from domestic violence?

Are you willing to lose your children to domestic violence?

How much has domestic violence cost you and your family? (money, property, health, employment, etc.)

What do you cover up after the abuse has occurred? (cover your face with makeup, lies to the kids, etc.)

Are drugs or alcohol involved?

____

____

____

____

Are you staying in an abusive relationship because you don't want to separate your family? Are you staying in an abusive relationship because you have no money? Are you staying in an abusive relationship because you have nowhere to go?

____

____

____

____

Are you staying in an abusive marriage because you don't want to get a divorce?

____

____

____

____

Abuse is not just about us. It's about our families, too. If you are a mother, I want you to think about your children. I would often wonder if I stayed what it would mean for my son. If I died, who would take care of him? If I stayed, what kind of man would he become? If I stayed, what was I demonstrating for him about how to treat and love women? If you think you are helping your children by staying, please think again. Children are like sponges, they absorb the abuse just as much as you do. You never know what effects the abuse may have on your children. They may grow up resenting you for staying. You could be the contributing factor of creating the next generation of abusers. My son witnessed some of my abuse and it left a permanent scar in his memory. Although my son is older now, he will never forget what happened. Talk to your children about what they've seen and heard and allow them to express themselves freely. Take them to therapy so they can talk through their feelings with a professional. But most importantly, please don't stay. Do it for them.

Let's continue to be honest with ourselves. Are you staying in an abusive relationship because you feel that your partner needs you? If so, what does your partner need from you that is so important you'll be beat for it? Have you ever thought about what he/she did before they met you?

____

____

____

____

You are not obligated to stay with anyone or anything against your will. Freedom comes at a cost. You will have to leave something to gain something. You will have to risk it all to save your life. How many times have we turned on the television or scrolled through our Facebook timelines and learned about a woman who had been murdered by a domestic partner? Those women didn't get a chance to get out. They too thought they would have one more time. They too thought they would call for help tomorrow.

Will you make that same mistake?

I'm so grateful to be able to say that chapter in my life is closed and I haven't looked back since. Thanks to God, my soul is free. Every day, I'm thankful that I have an opportunity to recover what was stolen from me: Love, Peace, and Happiness! I found true love from a man in the one place I hadn't looked—my father. After I left that abusive relationship, I had room in my heart for my father to come in and help me to understand the true meaning of love. I had to go back to my beginning so I could rewrite the end of this story. I didn't want to close the book as a victim. I wanted to be a heroine.

Who do you want to be in your story?

____

____

____

____

If you are a survivor of Domestic Violence, do you share your story? Why or Why not?

____

____

____

____

How do you feel when you relive your story?

____

How do you find peace again after you tell someone what has happened to you?

I tell my story because I know there are other women out there who need to hear it. The more I share that terrifying time in my life, I heal just a little bit more. My heart feels stronger and less bitter. I get control of my emotions. I grow. And I find purpose in knowing that I survived so I could share what happened to me with someone else. There are women in caskets and cemeteries all over the world right now who once walked in my shoes. I will scream my story from the rooftops and tell it a thousand times a day if I have to. My story is a part of me. It's my truth. And I'll continue to tell it, even when I get negative backlash from my abuser or his family. There is healing in truth.

Tell your truth today. Take your power back. I did it, and I am here as a living testament that you can do this. You deserve a life that is free from abuse. You deserve to be whole and healed and not broken. You are not worthless. You are not shattered beyond repair. You are not alone.

If you or someone you know are in an abusive relationship and need help contact the National Domestic Violence hotline @ 1-800-799-7233. Don't wait! You are not guaranteed to see another 24 hours of life.

You are too precious to be captive in an abusive relationship.

Too *Precious* to be…

Addicted

Your support system should never have the blood sucking trait of a leech.

We identify everything with a label.

If you look around, everything you use or consume—water, soap, and food—has a label. Movies are labeled as Rated R or MA or X. When we sit down to watch them, we shouldn't be surprised when there's nudity or compromising sexual situations. The label warned us.

We also use labels to classify individuals. If a person is a heavy drinker, they are labeled as an alcoholic. Someone who talks to themselves can be labeled as crazy. If they've been to jail, they are called a convict. When a person does too much of anything, we often label them as an addict. You can be addicted to almost anything, illegal drugs, prescription drugs, smoking, shopping, gambling, sugar, sex, or even those Thursday night high-drama shows we love to tune in for. Anything that demands your time, money, mental capabilities, and makes you feel that you can't live without it is your addiction.

And we all have one.

Hello, my name is Tokeitha and I am addicted to toxic relationships with men.

Wow. It's hard to write that. But it's such a reality for me. And sharing it with you frees me from the shame that comes with any addiction. It took me a long time to be honest with myself. For years I would stay in relationships that were unhealthy and poisonous to me. My fear of loneliness led me to and held me in so many unhealthy and poisonous relationships. I wanted to be hugged. I wanted to be loved. It was like a bottomless pit that could never be filled. So I tried to fill it with ugly relationships.

These relationships never gave me what I longed for. It was like going to a magic show in Vegas and being charmed and mesmerized by the enchanting acts, only to be robbed of everything afterwards. Just like each show has a review, so did each relationship. Some of the labels of my past relationships might read: Devil on a Pew, Its Hump Day, Deep Water, and the International Casanova Brown. You can tell I had a pretty interesting mix of men just from those labels. And the reviews? Even worse. None of them would be above two stars. But they felt so good in the moment. An addict just needs a taste. The idea of love kept me high.

I always had a man, and when I wasn't in a relationship I had a backup. My Plan B was always someone from the past who I could call on whenever I needed to. I had to sit in my loneliness because I never closed a door. To be honest, I dreaded ending a relationship and never really wanted to say "It's over" or "Goodbye." So for me, whenever a blast from the past would show up on my steps, it was like picking back up where we left off.

Spiritually, my lifestyle kept me in bondage. I settled for anything the wind decided to blow my way. Since I was always occupying my time with the wrong man, the right man could never find me. I was so blinded that I couldn't see anything clearly. My judgement in men was jaded. For an entire decade, I made bad choice after bad choice, suppressing my intuition and God's voice. I justified my addiction and hid behind the pleasure and lies that what I had was the love I needed. I only fooled myself.

What are you addicted to? (Be honest.)

____

____

____

____

How long have you been addicted? Years, months, days, or hours?

____

____

____

____

Addiction is a chemical romance. When you experience pleasure or happiness, your body rewards itself with small amounts of dopamine. Think about when you bite into a piece of chocolate and your taste buds go into a frenzy. Dopamine gives your body that same experience. When you step up your game and trade candy for heroin or cocaine, dopamine surges into your body. This is why you feel that high. Your body remembers everything you inject, inhale, or ingest. The more you give it, the more it wants.

My addiction left me feeling disconnected, lonely, and codependent. To get the attention and affection I craved, I allowed myself to be manipulated by the gifts, time spent, messages, dates, and trips. The cycle was vicious—I was high, but I was stressed, fatigued, and exhausted, too. When I tried to break free, I had withdrawals, anxiety, and cravings. I always just needed one more hit.

How has your addiction made you feel?

____

____

____

____

The first step to recovery is acceptance. You have to accept not just the addiction, but that you did not know the root cause of it. You couldn't control your body's response to what you tasted for the first time. You couldn't control your emotions on your own. Your behavior was a result of your heart's desire.

My dance with addiction didn't start with me and my intimate relationships. I am a Narcotic Anonymous baby. For years, I sat in meetings with my mother, watching her recovery process firsthand and the tenacity it took to get through it. It was a long, hard road for her but today she can celebrate over 25 years of sobriety. My mother is my shero and role model! She is a Warrior! She taught me if I took it one day at a time, I could get better.

Here are the keys to winning over your addiction to anything:

Pinpoint the cycle when it all started: Everything has a beginning. When you are trying to heal from addiction, you need to know what led you down the rabbit hole to begin with. Getting high—be it from drugs or anything else—was not the cause. That was the effect. But what got you there? Were you looking for love? Self-esteem? Did you watch a parent or someone you love drink? Think back over the years and look for your emotional patterns. If sex is your addiction, reflect on the times you had affairs or one-night stands, found yourself in a controlling relationship, or just sex. Go back to the times when you jumped from one man to the next and cracked the emergency glass on an ex or a "friend" just because. If you note your emotional state in each of those scenarios, you can likely trace your behavior to it. Now you can stop treating symptoms and get to the real issue.

Avoid anything that will trigger a relapse: Keep your temptations at bay so you are not tempted to give in to them. If you gamble, you wouldn't move next door to a casino or race track. If your vice is marijuana, don't go near anything that reminds or resembles the act of smoking, including such as a hookah, bongs, cigars, or even e-cigarettes. I had to completely sever all ties with men who weren't any good for me. No calls, no texts, no social media, nothing. Cold turkey.

Get a support system: Find loving, nurturing people who can walk beside you. Turn to your parents, friends, and a professional group to give you the encouragement you need to stay strong. Find that one friend who you can call in the middle of the night or day and she will pick up for you, no matter what. My best friend, Brandi, is that one for me. She has cried, fussed, cussed, intervened, and flat-out prayed for me. Every woman needs a friend like that in her life. My other close friends, Nikki and Michelle, complete my sister circle. These women fight for me and with me when I try to co-sign my own destruction. They love me enough to not allow me to wallow in my negativity. You need that.

Let go of your story: It's so easy for us to become addicted to our pasts and pain. We get comfortable with our labels—addict, alcoholic, liar, battered woman—whatever it is. As much as we want to be free, those titles become our identities. So we tell the same story over and over, not to help someone else, but because it's all we've known. Stop talking about those negative situations when they are not serving you. You are only resisting your recovery. Don't pollute your fresh start with poison from your past. I had to sever the cord to the drama in my life and stop feeding it by talking about what no longer existed. You should, too.

Who do you have in your corner to support you through recovery?

____

____

____

____

Can we get spiritual for just a minute? I want to talk to you about something that every woman has experienced at least once in her life. It's called the soul tie. Never heard of it? Or think maybe you've dodged that bullet? Let's see. You may be able to identify with something that happened to me.

I was in a relationship with a guy and I started to notice something weird happening. I could literally feel everything he felt. When he was sad, I was sad. If he had a craving for a certain food, so did I. Our intimacy and bond to one another surpassed sex. Our souls were joined, or tied, together. We were connected in every sense of the word—emotionally, spiritually, and physically. All of those texts, talks, promises, commitments, and intimacy kept me so intertwined with that guy that I couldn't shake him no matter how hard I tried.

Have you ever been there? Are you wondering why you feel so uncomfortable thinking about him months or even years after the breakup? Do the feelings make you confused and disgusted with yourself because you should be over him by now? You just want to move on with your life and be happy, but something is still there and you can't figure it out. (I know, boo. I've been there.) It's that familiar spirit he left you. That man is physically gone, yet you are full of his demons, including the ones passed down from generation to generation in his family. He was so suave and good looking that you didn't read his label. You thought you were just opening your legs, but you were really opening your soul.

Are you with me now, ladies?

Soul ties aside, how did we get there? How did we become addicts to relationships with men that don't nurture, love, and serve us back? I have been these girls before. Maybe you have, too:

The I-don't-want-him-but-I-don't-want-her-to-have-him girl: Have you stayed in a relationship far too long just because you didn't want to let go? Sometimes we purposefully hold on to men to prevent them from moving on. We know they aren't the man for us, yet we don't want them with anyone else. We give away everything we have, including our dignity and our bodies, to hold on to something that (a) isn't good for us, and (b) was never meant to be ours. Let it go.

The I'll-do-anything-to-keep-him girl: How often do we bend over backwards for unworthy men and relationships? As women we have to stop lowering ourselves. Don't leave your morals at the door and drop your panties once the door is closed. We've all been there.

The Every-Guy-Is-The-One girl: Is every man you meet the man of your dreams? I suffered from The Perfect Guy syndrome for years. Every time I thought I found Mr. Right, he turned out to be Mr. All The Way Wrong. I was lured in by what I wanted to see and not by what's real. I fell in love with the idea of a fantasy—the prince, the white horse, the white dress, the glistening diamond ring—but what was the reality? A man who glittered like gold on the outside but his gas tank was on empty on the inside. I didn't take the time to get to know, learn, observe, or research the men who came into my life. And I made the mistake more than once.

It became clear that it was more about me and my choices then the men I dated. When we keep the same type of dude over and over again, we have to step back and examine ourselves. We want and need love, but we have to start seeking it from the right sources. We have to stop being so willing with our hearts, souls, and bodies. We have to stop allowing our addictions to drive us to make poor choices.

As women, we lead with our hearts and our bodies first. But does he deserve either? Every man that enters into our bodies carries emotion, disease, and all of the other women he has entered with him. So when we find ourselves battling depression, loneliness, low self-esteem and suicidal thoughts, it's because of all of that old baggage was left inside. Just like the trash man dumping the garbage in the local landfill, a man can do the same. One man can cause you to lose it. The more men we allow in, we only increase our risks.

But, ladies, we can't put all of the blame on the men. We bring our garbage, too. And we've ruined some good men as a result. Let's start taking the time to deal with our stuff. Take a timeout. You owe it to yourself. It's worth the investment of time to seek therapy, build and strengthen a relationship with God, and even money for a short restoration vacation if that's what you need. Find a way to feel better about yourself so you can show in a relationship as your best self, and not a broken version of the original.

I couldn't encourage you or share these experiences if I hadn't been there. It wasn't until I hit rock bottom one day that my addictions became clear to me. Something just came over me and I knew I couldn't continue to live the same way. I had to figure out how to dig myself out from the hole I was in. My tolerance level had reached its peak. I didn't want to overindulge in men anymore. I didn't want to chase relationships and invest all of my time, energy, and self to get nothing in return. I didn't want to allow loneliness and my addiction to toxic love rule my life anymore. Finally, I had enough.

Have you hit rock bottom? If yes, what are your breaking point(s)?

____

____

____

____

If you haven't hit rock bottom, how much longer will it take for you to see how your addiction has affected you?

____

____

____

____

God took control. He knew what I needed. I refer to that season of my life as The Breaking. God broke every facet of my life into small pieces. Every level and layer was broken. He broke me in so many ways that it was only His grace and mercy that could have kept me. I started to seek Him feverishly. I accepted GOD into my life to repair me from the abuse and the toxic relationships and He began to work on me as if He had been waiting for me to come. He removed every distraction from my life, and I obeyed by devoting my time and energy to give Him what He wanted from me. I owed God. In fact, I was like that overdue credit card; He kept calling me, but I didn't want to answer. But when I accepted the call and said yes, I immediately went to a higher place in my life.

I didn't change overnight and it wasn't some hocus pocus either. It requires discipline every day. Trust me when I say, I get tempted. But I ask God first to help me read the labels of the men I meet and to give me the discernment to see clearly. I seek and ask Him through prayer, even at 5:00 a.m.

As I got reacquainted with God, I made a conscious effort to become a new me. I got comfortable with being alone. No longer would I wear the label "lonely." My new way of thinking was simple: being alone didn't mean lonely. I removed the blinders so I could see clearly. I set boundaries for the first time in a really long time. Saying "No" was cool again and I loved it. You should practice it: "No, No," and my favorite, "Didn't I just say NO!" It feels good.

I was determined that my foundation would be stronger and each level of me would be structurally stable. I would no longer allow the wind to blow whatever it wanted my way. Like my bestie would say, "I am addicted to my happiness." I wasn't going to stay in any relationship that was toxic to me. In fact, if I so much as smell or sense any level of toxicity or negativity, I'm out.

What was the outcome of your breaking? What will you do differently?

____

____

____

____

How do you feel about yourself now that change has occurred?

____

____

____

____

Most addicts credit God at some point in their recovery. I am no different. You may hear a person reflect on how God's grace kept them from destruction. For me, I would have nothing if it wasn't for His grace and mercy upon me. Before, I wanted my way no matter the cost. Although it was not always good, I had a self-destructive mindset. I lived a decade of my life feeling like I was all alone and I tried to replace the void with man after man. There was only one man who made it, so today I am here to tell you this story in good health. That is none other than GOD.

If you are suffering from addiction or know of someone who is, please get help. Don't feel alone, you can always accept GOD into your life. For me, it was as simple as ABC:

A-I accepted the Lord Jesus Christ into my life.

B-I believe in my heart the Lord Jesus Christ died for me and my sins.

C-I confess with my mouth and I repent of my sins because I'm a child of GOD. My sins are forgiving in Jesus' name. I'm saved!

Be honest with yourself and accept who you are. Yes you have some negative behavior patterns and you've made some bad decisions, but you don't have to stay in that place. Realize that you have the power and ability to overcome your habits. Get on the road to recovery and restore yourself. Get around the right people who support you and believe in you!

For professional help with narcotic or alcohol addiction, contact the Addiction Treatment Hotline at 1-888-827-7180. You can also find Narcotics Anonymous online at www.na.org and Alcoholics Anonymous at www.aa.org.

If you need assistance for gambling addictions, contact the National Council on Problem Gambling at 1(800)522-4700.

For Sexual Addiction visit Sexual Addiction Anonymous at www.saa-recovery.org or call at 1(800)477-8191.

For Overeaters Anonymous visit www.oa.org

For immediate assistance, contact the Crisis Hotline at 1(800)273-8255.

You are too precious to be addicted!

Too *Precious* to be...

Embarrassed

Nothing about you is generic.

There are 7 deadly sins: Lust, Sloth, Envy, Wrath, Greed, Gluttony, and, one of my favorites to discuss, Pride. I have committed them all. More than likely you have, too. Even when our sins seem small, they're still there. But pride has caught me up in its web more times that I can count. Pride manifests in so many forms— arrogance, vanity, and conceitedness to name a few. Pride feeds the ego and keeps you from admitting your mistakes. Pride refuses to allow you to accept the truth. Pride kills relationships and separates families. Like a cancer, pride shows up in your mental, physical, financial, and spiritual life. Prides covers the truth.

Like the best concealer money can buy, pride disguises flaws and the things we don't want the world to see. It covers all of our flaws and imperfections. Pride is so sneaky. It convinces us that no one should know when we fall. We don't want to be uncomfortable, so we keep anything that doesn't match the face we put out for everyone to see locked and hidden away.

Pride leads us to put more emphasis on the feeling than the fact. If something ugly happens to us or we find ourselves in a bad situation unexpectedly, we assume people will judge us without knowing for sure. We lose sight of the fact that our families, friends, and those who truly care about us know our hearts, and accept us with our flaws and all. Yet too often, we sit in silence, gripped by the fear of humiliation.

Think of an incident or situation that made you feel gross, nasty, disgusted, shocked, uncivilized, disrespected, or appalled. Then answer the questions below.

What have you participated in that you are most embarrassed about?

____

____

____

____

How did it make you feel before, during, and afterwards?

Before

____

____

____

____

During

____

____

____

____

Afterwards

____

____

____

____

Was someone or something harmed from your decision?

____

____

____

____

How long and how often did you allow this to happen?

____

____

____

Sometimes we get embarrassed at work. It could be due to messing up a presentation or an assignment our boss gives us. It happens when we get caught doing something we know we shouldn't do, like stealing or lying on our timesheets. And then there are those office romances, the ones that lead to all of our personal business being buzzed about everywhere from the hallways to happy hour to human resources. Many of us have found ourselves in these compromising and very embarrassing scenarios.

Disclaimer: This is my opinion and I am sticking to it.

The office relationship should be forbidden at all costs. I know some people have met the loves of their lives at work and skipped off into the sunset together, but I would be willing to bet that those instances are few and far between. Relationships at work create so much conflict in the workplace. It can be fine if kept between the two people involved, but the problem comes in when others want to know the big secret. Depending on the players—two peers or an employee and a manager—things could get extra messy. Let's not forget the extra time booed up at the copier, at lunch, or a quick smoke break. (Is it me or do smokers get the best of both worlds on the job? I digress). My point is it's rare for a workplace romance to end up with a happily ever after.

Think I may have a little experience in this area? You would be right. I'll share a bit if you don't mind? Good.

He was tall, dark, and handsome. We often worked together on projects and near each other. The attraction was almost instant. We started with small talk and found out that we had a lot in common. We were even the same zodiac sign.

We had the best lunch dates! We both were young and single so dating and getting to know each other was fun. The more time we spent together, the more our feelings for each other grew. That's when the whispers started. People in the office became intrusive and questioned me about the details of my relationship. One supervisor even pulled me into her office to question me and him on separate occasions. What started out as something so innocent and fun between us became complicated and stressful. Although I didn't owe anyone any explanations about my personal life, I started to feel guilty despite the fact that I was doing nothing wrong.

I felt so uncomfortable.

Fast forward down memory lane, I got pregnant. As the gossip grew, so did my belly. People begin to speculate about the father of my unborn child. Whose baby was I carrying? Everyone wanted to know. I blocked the negativity. I embraced my pregnancy, and enjoyed every minute of it. Eventually, the father and I separated due to a jail sentence, but I held on to my happiness even though he was no longer there to hold me at lunchtime, be at the doctor's appointments, or watch our favorite team play on Sunday.

One afternoon, a manager pulled me into her office. She politely closed the door and sat at her desk. She folded her hands, looked me in the eyes, and asked, "Tokeitha, is that baby by…?" I was stunned. I couldn't believe we were having this conversation. Never in million years did I think that my personal life would be the discussion of a government agency. Yet it was and still is to this day. I never broke any rules at work. I never broke up a marriage or family. We never kissed or anything else in the office. Why did I feel like I was being punished? I felt so ashamed.

When I returned from maternity leave, I bought the hurt of that gossip and ridicule right back with me. A new mother to a beautiful son, I couldn't share the experience with any co-workers. I didn't want to fuel the fire and, besides, I felt like I couldn't trust anyone. I never put pictures of my child on my desk. But I still got to celebrate my son in a different way. A relative worked in the same office and she covered her cubicle with photos of my baby. People were always puzzled by how excited I got whenever I passed her desk and saw a new picture. Like all women, we had something in common. Over the years no one knew we were in love with the same person. A little boy name Messiah.

I refused to allow pride to steal my joy. This was just one instance in my life when the threat of embarrassment would have wreaked serious havoc in my life if I had let it. Yes, it showed up, but I wasn't going to give into it. I had my moments when I shed tears, when I prayed to God for understanding, when I called friends and families in despair because I couldn't understand why people who didn't even know me would make up lies about me and my life. But I wasn't going to just give in. I was a grown woman with the right to make her own choices and decisions. The End. If I had been too proud to own my relationship and my son, I would have been compelled to explain myself to strangers give up my good, government job or maybe even give up my son for fear that somebody was talking about me. Pride could have cost me so much.

When has pride cost you something or someone that you loved?

____

____

____

Pride and embarrassment could be a barricade to your next blessing. Being afraid to worship, praise, or give thanks are all examples of this. You should never be too high and superior that you can't be thankful. Some people feel embarrassed about their religions, faith, or beliefs when they are around others who may not share the same sentiments. Own your God and what you believe. Stand firm.

How many families have been ripped apart by pride? Funerals are filled with relatives and friends who never got that apology they deserved or couldn't reconnect with someone before they passed away. People die too embarrassed to admit their mistakes and shortcomings and now it's too late. Don't let pride kill your family. If you have a family member that you haven't talked to in years, call them or reach out to them. Keep trying even if they don't respond or you don't receive the graciousness or any sign of remorse. Your trying is not in vain. Sometimes you have to do it for you. And sometimes people do come back around and acknowledge their mistakes. That manager who called me into her office and tried to humiliate me? Well, years later, she apologized. I could have flew off the handle on her, but I didn't. I wasn't too prideful to accept her sincerity and she didn't allow pride to stand in the way of her doing the right thing. We were both women and could respect each other.

Are there any situations in your life were you can resolve an issue, whether it's on the job, family, or church? If so, how will you reconnect with someone and what will you do differently next time?

____

____

____

____

Too *Precious* to be...

Struggling

A woman wears many hats
A woman earns many shoes
But she only gives from her one heart

One of the most demanding and rewarding titles is Mother. When a woman births a child, she is a walking illustration of humbleness. Yet she is confident and assured. Motherhood places demands on your time in every sense, mentally, physically, spiritually, and financially. Mothers nurturer and smother simultaneously. Mothers are the women who defy all odds to become trendsetters, game changers, icons, and role models while raising healthy, smart, and loving children. With all that she gives and does, to her children and the world, a mother should never struggle.

When I became a mother, I began to fully understand the magnitude of my responsibility. As a child, you don't realize the incredible sacrifices a mother makes. It's so easy to take our mothers for granted, at least I did. I focused more on her mistakes and missteps than I did her greatness, her goodness, and everything she's done for me all of my life. It took having a child of my own to fully appreciate her. I remember the stress and heartache I caused her. I remember her prayers and tears. I remember the roofs over my head (the one-bedroom apartment all the way to the house with my own room). I remember riding the bus and walking because we did not have a car. I remember every day she prayed morning and at night. My mother sacrificed so much for me. In her trials and eventually her triumphs, my mother showed me what a mother should be. My mother taught me a lot of things, especially how to sacrifice and how to push through.

My son pushed me harder than ever before in life. When I got pregnant, I was two classes away from completing my Masters of Science in Public Health. I failed and could not get back into the school, even after three appeals. It would ultimately take me seven years to complete my degree program. In fact, my son and I graduated together. I received a Master of Public Health and my son went onto the first grade.

Before my son was born, I was warned that I would have to sacrifice and struggle, but it all became a reality from the moment he was placed in my arms. I had degrees, but I didn't earn enough to live comfortably without worry or financial stress. I had a mortgage, student loans, and a car note—now I had childcare and baby necessities added to the load.

I watch the news and read books on my smartphone because childcare comes before cable television. I pack my son's lunch or pay out of pocket because I am ineligible for the free or reduced lunch program due to my on-paper income. Then there's everyday life costs like gas (I look forward to winters when gas is so much cheaper) and maintenance for the car, dry cleaning expenses, and his extracurricular activities.

A mother's sacrifice is so serious. Providing for our children and keeping them safe drives us. We have to make due and survive. It's not about us. It's about them. So you clean your one mattress that the children urinate on every day so that your house doesn't smell. You stretch the food so that everyone can eat but you. You put in the extra hours and hold your emotions in check at work so that you can keep your job. You keep that one good outfit clean and neat so that you can feel good about yourself when you step out into the world. You negotiate with the mechanic and the utility company so the electric isn't disconnected. We are fixers, snow shovelers, grass cutters—and we do it without selling or using our bodies to get what we need for our families. Somehow, it all gets done. We work miracles as mothers.

We are warriors, even in the struggle.

What are some of your everyday struggles?

____

____

____

____

What are the barriers that keep you from moving past the struggles?

____

____

____

What are the resources needed to remove the barrier (education, transportation, finances, etc.)?

____

____

____

____

I wear my struggles as a badge of honor. There are many other mothers, like me, who have less than I have and make it happen. We're in this together. We pray for one another and we lift each other up. So our struggles are more meaningful than we know. Think about this:

Behind every struggle there is purpose. Our sacrifice today is what will propel our children to their next level of greatness. When you sit next to a mother at a graduation, honor roll program, or wedding with those tears streaming down her cheeks, she is reminded of everything it took to get there. Her cries of frustration and pain, her making-a-way-outta-no-way, her giving everything she had was all worth it. That's what it is all about. So don't give up in midst of the struggle. Push through to the other side.

Behind every struggle there is an opportunity to be more grateful. Mothers are too precious to struggle, but we do. This is why it's so important to ask for help when we need it, and to accept it when it comes. If a set of helping hands comes your way, grab them. If someone you know offers you money or some other form of help, don't be proud. Accept that blessing! Some never receive any support, so be gracious and grateful when you do.

I am thankful for everyone, especially the women, who have blessed and supported me along my motherhood journey. I had Mrs. Cynthia who would call me every day at 5:00 am so that I could make it to work on time. My mentor, Lisa, who told me I have to keep going because the next generation needs me. First Lady White and her power of prayer saw me through time and time again. Mrs. Saddler's wise words of choice during our hair sessions and Ms. Jackson sent me spontaneous checks in the mail. I am even grateful for the Obama Administration! I have a home, a job thanks to the Affordable Care Act, and my student loans are eligible for a forgiveness program. My son has been to the White House four times!

I know you have blessings to be grateful for, too.

Behind every struggle is joy. Often it's the little things that make us smile. A moment of laughter will break all of the stress up into tiny pieces (Am I the only mom who stays cracking up at her kid?) Always look for the joy in every struggle you endure. The storm doesn't last always. The purpose of this struggle could be to encourage you to let more joy into your life.

What brings you joy?

____

____

____

Life as a mother has so many obstacles. But, as mothers, we've all walked this same path. Renew your strength and your faith in God right now. Thank Him for what He's done and for the promises you're waiting for Him to deliver. Thank Him for the hard stuff. Get to a place where you can truly say, "Thank you, God," with a pure heart. Our children are watching us. When it gets hard for you, think of them. Lean on them, too. When I am having a horrible day, a hug and kiss from my son makes things right again. Find the strength when you need it.

Always remember you are too precious to struggle.

Too *Precious* to be...

Captive

Change happens twice a day:
Day
Night

Every offender who has entered into a prison or incarceration of any kind has been gripped by bondage. There were shackles or handcuffs, an officer dictating how they would live, what time to sleep and wake up, and what time to eat. My mother was locked up when I was five years old; my father was incarcerated almost my entire life, so I know this life all too well, even from the outside.

As a kid, I remember it all. The bus rides to the jail to visit. The jailhouse doors slamming behind me and the long lines and the pat down from strangers. I recall what felt like a few seconds to talk through thick glass on a phone. Every time I would leave my mother, I would put my small hand up to the glass to say goodbye and she would put her hand in the same spot.

That was the only prison life I knew. Until I grew up.

We think of prison behind bars, but we can be confined in any facet of our lives. We can live in the clutches of fear, a lack of passion, and lives and people we don't love. Yes, prison doesn't have to be a cell. Our minds can keep us caged, too.

What about jails like:

Your Relationship: Your mate keeps cheating on you. He's given you a Sexually Transmitted Infection or Disease, disrespected you in every way possible, and there is no chance of commitment. But you stay because you love him.

Your Job: You hate going to work in the morning. Every performance evaluation is exactly the same—negative. You should be somewhere, doing something else. But you won't apply for another job.

Your Place of Worship: You go to that same church every single Sunday; it's your family's tradition. You don't love it and you're not growing spiritually. But you won't search for a new church home.

Your House: You are trying to stay sober and on the right track. Your neighborhood tempts you to drink or do drugs every time you walk outside. But you won't move.

Your Money: You need approval and to look good to the world. You live above your means, your credit cards are maxed out. You're broke. But you won't stop spending and ask for help.

Do you see how we can be confined in our minds? Our minds can either hold us captive or free us. Some of us are so far removed from freedom and restricted by our minds, lives, and decisions that we feel caged. I've been there—trapped in a life that I didn't love. It's like wearing a boa constrictor around your neck. The snake is steadily squeezing and squeezing until you have no breath left. You want to breathe, but your circumstances, or your perception of them, are holding you captive.

Do you feel that you are a prisoner in your mind? If yes, describe the feeling(s) of confinement you have?

____

____

____

____

What is it that makes you feel confined (employment, relationship, religion, residence, class, family, etc)?

____

____

____

____

How long have you felt confined (List the type of confinement and the amount of time [years, months, days, hours, etc.])? Example: Relationship/12 years

____

____

____

____

Are you in denial? Do you think that you're exempt from negativity? Are you perfect?

____

____

____

____

Have you become immune to positivity and prefer to stay in self-pity, heartbreak, low self-esteem? Think about how you got to this point of acceptance.

____

____

____

____

Are you ready to break free? Here's how:

Clean House

Freedom begins with taking the trash out in your life. That's right, just like taking out the garbage in your household, you have to remove the garbage in your mind. Your digestive system purges and cleanses every day; your thoughts need to do the same. Learn to let go and remove the garbage and wasteful thinking. Watch and witness the difference in your mind and in your life.

Activate Your Faith

Your mind is a powerful weapon, and with the right tools, you can escape your very own prison sentence. For me, my first step was to activate my faith. I started where I was, praying and becoming intimate with GOD. Faith is a relative of hope. We often hear the biblical example of faith being the size of a mustard seed. A mustard seed is 1 to 2 mm in size. That is very tiny to the eye, but, like any seed, once it's planted and watered, it can grow. So when you build enough faith in yourself to escape your prison sentence, you have just planted a seed.

Nurture Your Faith

Every seed needs to be watered. The watering process is the critical phase. You have to discipline yourself to continue to move forward. Freedom in your mind comes by viewing life differently and using your peripheral view. Stop thinking that your future is one-dimensional; there is so much more in store. There are all types of views— widescreen, full screen, and panoramic. Go for the full view. Let go of the coulda-woulda-shoulda moments of your past. Start with today and move into the I shall have, I shall receive, and I shall give moments life has to offer.

Think Affirming Thoughts

Every time you feel those negative, trashy thoughts attempting to reemerge, turn them into positive thoughts of hope. Give yourself an injection of confidence and self-worth by accepting that you have control over your life. Decide how you want to live, play, eat, and sleep.Write it down.Your mind and eyes will start to connect to the vision. Your spirit will be renewed with the energy to continue to move forward.

Put a timeline on it

Set specific dates and goals for your escape. I have a number of short-term goals that I have set for myself, and I typically create them in 30 day increments. For long-term goals, I may stretch them to annually, five years, and ten years.

Visualize the vision

I use pictures, words, figures to capture the image in my mind. I have a vision, and I look at it every day. I have multiple vision boards and I even created a visual vision for this book. This helps my body to encompass where I want to go. The vision is embedded into my mind for the future. My vision is detailed. It illustrates every aspect of my life. Just like a Fortune 500 company, you need a vision.

How do you see your future? When you answer that question think about your life fully, in every dimension.

Create your own vision book, vision board, or vision screenshot. Use images of businesses, exotic places, salary figures, and partnerships representing everything you want in your life. Post it in areas that you spend lots of time like the car, home, and work. Mediate on it.

In my home, I have a Wall of Fame. We pass it whenever we go up or down the stairs. I have both of my degrees on display in the middle of the wall, yet my son's awards are surrounding my degrees. I would like to see my son degrees replace mine one day and continue our family's legacy of Morehouse men and Bennett women. This is simple but it leaves a lasting impression. The wall reminds us to continue to work toward achievement. It's also a conversational piece as my son expresses to me how many awards he has. He says to me, "Mommy, you need to catch up because I have more than you." He has so many awards that I always have to purchase frames for him. I'm so proud of my little guy.

Here's the point. Keep your vision in front of you.

As your visuals begin to take shape, ask yourself, is

my vision clear? There are still obstacles in life that may cause interference and blur your vision. You could be unable to see things clearly or be completely blinded. Then there is the obstructive view—only being able to see part of what's around you. You may have tunnel vision at times, and it may actually be necessary to keep you focused and moving in the right direction. All of these views will come into play as you are executing your vision and your plan. When you are blurry, adjust your lens and get clear. If there is something in the way of your vision, remove it. If you need less distraction, turn up the tunnel vision. Do what you need to do to stay on target.

I challenge you to write out your great escape. Include what you will do daily, monthly, and yearly. Include how you will counter the negativity. How will you remove the wasteful thinking? How often will you purge? How will you escape from your prison sentence?

____

____

____

____

____

____

____

____

____

____

After writing your plan, refuse to not go back to that jailed mindset. Stay disciplined and committed to your plan. The freedom of your mind is priceless. Your mind is like a new car—you have to get routine maintenance to keep it running smoothly. Remember your seed must be watered in order to grow. Don't stop wanting to be better. Don't stop having hope and faith in yourself. You shall move out of your current state of mind and have the power to overcome. You shall have faith to achieve everything that you envision. You are too precious to be in jail. You are too precious to be confined.

You are too precious to be captive. Free your mind!

Too *Precious* to be...

Unhealthy

....

Life requires you to touch, taste, smell, see, and hear all that it has in store for you.

When you purchase a new car, it comes with the tags and removable plastic linings on it. The car is shiny and new, and all it needs is a wash from time to time, gas, and an oil change to keep it running beautifully. But over time that new car smell begins to go away. The car starts to huff and puff a bit. It needs more extensive work and a lot of TLC to stay operational. Your body is like that new car.

We all want to be healthy and live long lives for our children and our families, right?

Maintaining you starts with these steps:

See a doctor

Making appointments with your doctor for annual exams and routine health screenings for diseases like diabetes and hypertension. For health conditions like obesity, there are more extensive treatments, such as gastric bypass surgery, that may be needed to improve our health. Sitting down with a physician is an opportunity to discuss any health challenges and a treatment plan to address them. Do whatever it takes.

Many of us refuse to see a doctor out of fear. We can see an abnormal growth growing or have a pain, but we won't find out what's wrong. Those are indicators and signals. Don't allow ignorance to lead to a disease, or worse kill you. You're too precious to be unhealthy.

Keep it moving

Exercise is critical to your overall health. You have to move! If you need accountability and one-on-one motivation, invest in a personal trainer. Local gyms have Zumba and spin classes. More neighborhoods are including bike lanes along with trails for increased activity. So we all can get in shape somehow someway.

Eat well

As a child, I remember going to the market with my grandmother getting fresh fruits and vegetables by the crate. She cooked every day during the week and all day on the weekends. She fed the entire neighborhood fresh greens, string beans, peach cobbler, and bread. On Saturday mornings we would go to the market and local grocery stores. We ate fresh all the time. We rarely ate out, especially fast food. Follow my grandmother's example and eat healthy, fresh foods. Cook good meals at home and enjoy them with your family.

Eat smart

Nothing was wasted in my grandmother's house; leftovers were always turned into a soup. Plan your meals, too. Think about how you can save money by using food multiple ways. You won't get bored and you'll have healthier food choices. Chronic conditions like high blood pressure, diabetes and high cholesterol can also be controlled or avoided by diet.

Know your medical history

Our medical history is just like a CarFax—its critical information that we need to know. When we know conditions run in our family, we can begin to prepare and prevent a cycle of disease. Ignorance and lack of proper education keeps us in the wrong state of mind. You will always be in bondage if you are ignorant to the facts.

Avoid the gimmicks and shortcuts

Health and fitness is a wealthy industry. You name it, it's on the market. You can always find the latest greatest exercise program, supplements, and equipment. But figure out what you actually need, what's best for you, and invest in those things.

These days you can supersize everything including your appearance. Men and women can get injections and implants to enhance their features. But cosmetic surgery can be dangerous, especially if it's not done by a professional. A friend's cousin recently passed away from illegal butt injections. I heard a story of a successful entrepreneur that died from complications of a tummy tuck. Some people die on the table, floor, or where ever the procedure is being administered. Sometimes we may think we are getting a good deal, but the reality is a bootleg surgery or a black market price kills. We all have to be smart about our health. Don't take risks with your body. Just like any major purchase, do your research and compare. Look at board certified and malpractice claims. Don't make a decision you could regret.

With all of the temptations for fast and instant results, we have to discipline ourselves. We are accountable for our own actions and that includes our health. I am running this health race right alongside you! I know as women and mothers, we have a tough time putting ourselves first at times. I have those same challenges. I have a few tips for you to help you stay focused and to manage your overall health better.

Time Management:

Like you I have a hard time getting myself together. Time management is my biggest hurdle. I had to learn to schedule my time in order to maximize my day. I schedule days and time to do assignments and for family time, writing, meetings, and exercise. It can be complicated to create a schedule and to stick to it, but I don't want to be unhealthy. If I don't take my health seriously and I get sick, everything around me could fall and crumple. Who will take care of my son, pay the bills, and keep food on the table? The same goes for you.

Accountability:

I've found that I need to be held accountable. My family and friends help me with this. I know it's real when I start to receive old pictures of myself when I was pounds lighter. Yes, my mother, sister, and bestie are the keepers of the throwback pictures. They remind me when I'm gaining weight or action needs to be taken. We also workout together; it helps to have a partner. We go to the gym, turn on the music, and get moving. We push each other to keep going.

Mindset:

Your mindset is the major component to staying healthy. It's a daily fight to eat the right food, exercise, and maintaining a healthy lifestyle. It's a mind game every day, from the enticing food on the commercial to the bright colors waking your senses. Your mind is like that car with the computer chip full of sensors. I try to eliminate as much of those teasers as possible. I am so determined when I want to lose weight; the pounds don't even stand a chance.

Resources:

There are so many resources available to receive healthcare in order to live a healthy lifestyle. Free health events are found on social media platforms promoting the health screenings and resources. More people are able to receive health insurance as a result of the Affordable Care Act. So we all have to work toward living a healthy lifestyle so that we can live longer.

Getting Your Mind Right

Mental and Behavioral health is just as important as our physical health. Mental health has been all over the headlines recently. It seems that more and more people are suffering from mental illnesses and going undiagnosed or untreated. This, as we know, can be dangerous and deadly. When people don't get the help they need, they can possibly harm themselves or others.

Bipolar disorder is often associated with mood swings feelings of highs and lows in life. Feelings of worry and panic can be signals of depression or anxiety. So many people suffer from Post-Traumatic Stress Disorder (PTSD), as a result of witnessing a terrifying event. You could be experiencing any of these symptoms and so could a spouse, child, or relative who is suffering. If your mood has changed drastically, talk to a professional for help.

How would you rate your health?

Unsatisfactory
Poor
Average

Above Average

How can you improve your health?

____

____

____

____

How can you improve your children's health?

____

____

____

____

What can you do at home if a gym membership is not affordable?

____

____

____

____

What household items can you use to create an exercise program? (i.e., Cans, Broom Sticks, Chairs)

____

What are your favorite songs to listen to while working out?

What are 3 things you can live without for the next 30 days in order to improve your health?

What diseases and conditions are linked to your family history? Breakdown the medical history.
Grandparents:

Parents:

Siblings:

Do you have any known mental illnesses in your family? If so list them.

Have you educated your children on the importance of each diseases and/or conditions in your family? Why or why not?

____

____

____

There comes a time when you have to make your health a priority. We owe it to ourselves to be the best. As parents, we want the best for our children; we have to want the same for ourselves.

Remember you're that car that needs to run smooth despite the number of miles. Our bodies are equipped with the proper tools which keep us in optimal health. Our heart is like an engine; it's fast and constantly at work. Our brain is like the electrical system; without it, "Houston we have a problem!" Our lungs are like the air filter and our kidneys are like the oil filter. The filters always have to be clean. Our digestive system is like the exhaust; it removes the waste. Our skin must stay clean just like the car being waxed and paint protected. Our eyes are the headlights to see what direction we are going. Lastly, every car needs fluids; we need water to stay hydrated.

So I challenge you to do better. Start today by going to your doctor and knowing your health status. Ask questions if you don't know. Learn about new ways to improve your health.

You are too precious to be unhealthy!

Too *Precious* to be...

Fatherless

Every lesson learned in life is not verbal. Observation can be a lifesaver.

When I think of a mythical creature, the first one that comes to my mind is a phoenix. A phoenix is symbolic in religion and also in Greek mythology. The bird's significance is that it arises from the ashes and brings new life. The phoenix has a spirit of resilience and power. A phoenix represents rejuvenation and renewal. A phoenix is everything a woman is supposed to be—warm, bold, and confident.

Like the phoenix, I have a boldness and resilience in my spirit that I inherited from my parents. Some of it I had to pick up along the journey of the life they created for me. Like the phoenix I arose from the ashes. Not just any ashes, the ashes of a prison. Conceived in Lorton Federal Penitentiary, I was too precious to be fatherless.

I didn't know much about my father, except for the legendary stories I'd heard about his exceptional intelligence and smooth demeanor. According to family and neighborhood folklore, my father was "The Man." He was a powerful man, even in prison. He had control over many of the correctional officers because they were on his payroll. I was told that my father had an office in prison and ran an enterprise that was so major it was featured on the local news and even on *20/20*. He would also arrange private visits with my mother while he was in jail—another testament to the commanding man he was. Lorton was known for corruption, embezzlement, fraud, and all kinds of illegal activities went on inside. My father could do everything he did on the outside if he wanted to.

Stories are great, but there is nothing like having your father in your life. My brother and I suffered growing up without him or any father figure for years. My brother was ten years older than me and we were both raised by our grandmothers and aunts. I met my brother once during my childhood. Our father took us skating at the local skating rink, Crystals. Crystals is that place where everyone went to show off their skills. My only memory of us ever being together was at the skating rink having a blast.

I have other memories of my father that I've pieced together throughout my life. I most vividly remember the disappointment and my mother having to make amends for his false promises. I would wait by the window, hoping that he would show up like he promised. He wouldn't, and my mother would be furious that he let me down again. I remember every one of those tears, and asking questions like, "Why isn't he here? How much longer do I have to wait? What did I do wrong?" Those are questions that no child should ever have to ask a parent.

I always remember my father with a woman. The few times we were together, there would be another woman with us. I can count on one hand each encounter. When I got older, I began to understand. My father was a ladies' man; always has been and always will be. The father that I knew put everything before me, especially the women. Apparently he was easy to love. I wish I knew how to love him.

Are you a fatherless child? ___________

Was your father present in your life? If so, how long has he been in your life (years, months, days)?

____

____

____

____

Describe your emotions as a result of growing up in a fatherless environment?

____

____

____

____

I never asked to be fatherless, but I was. As a young girl, I had friends that grew up with both parents. Their mothers and fathers would come to games, PTA meetings, and musical performances to support them and cheer them on from the sidelines or audience. My mother couldn't always attend my school activities because she had to work. But she did her best to recognize my accomplishments.

Eventually, my brother and I both had male figures come into our lives who could nurture and guide us. When my mother married my stepfather, he became my daddy. For the first time, I had a two- parent household. My daddy was such a blessing to me. That man had to be God sent to both me and my mom; I was so defiant and resistant to him at first. It had been just me and my mother for so long, and the idea of sharing her with someone else did not sit well with me initially. I was mean to him. In fact, I intentionally did things to make it difficult in their relationship. While they were dating, I would act all the way out—leaving him on hold when he called for my mom, not telling her he was at the door when he came to pick her up for dates, the whole nine. (I told you I was a Smart Aleck, right?). Thankfully this man had the patience of Job.

Our breakthrough came when he saved my life, at least as far as I'm concerned. I got in trouble at school, and instead of calling my mother, I called my stepdad. I begged him not to tell my mom. After making me promise to never do it again, he agreed to keep my secret. That day, my daddy made a commitment to be there for me and he has been there every day since. We've been through our growing pains, but he loved me from the start and that has never changed. I can always talk to my dad about anything, at any time, and he always listens to me. His advice is priceless.

After all, I'm too precious to be fatherless.

Not only do I have my daddy, but I am fathered by many other men in my life. I have a network of fathers. These men are equivalent to the team that Olivia Pope has on Scandal—they are my gladiators. There is Mr. Saddler, my best friend Brandi's dad, who is always available and the first man I call when my daddy is unavailable. Mr. Saddler is like a conductor; he handles all things electrical and makes sure I stay plugged into life. Then there is Mr. Owens, my best friend Nikki's dad. I call him when I need to talk numbers, money, or financial strategies. Pastor Kevin, the Pastor of New Life Christian Center Church, always shows up for me—from the courtroom to the awards ceremony. With PK on the scene, I can count on being introduced to someone of importance that he knows. He is the networker. I can't forget Mr. Siegel and Mr. Davis who are both retired and living life. I turn to them for intellectual insight and literature. They are two of my strongest supporters, rooting for me every step of the way.

My gladiators have helped me to fight some of my toughest battles.When my back was against the wall, they were there. They are all valuable, not only to me but to this world. They are rich in wisdom, humor, and all things women. They teach me not to panic, to be patient, and most of all, to stay cool. With the exception of a few, we all are football fans of the same team. So when it's all said and done we can talk football. Just like my daddy taught me.

In the end, God gave me more fathers than I could ever ask for or need. Starting with Him.

Who was the father figure in your life? What made him so unique or special to you?

____

____

____

Describe your most memorable moment about your father, daddy, or father figure in your life?

____

____

____

____

Over the years, my father and I have tried to work on our relationship. Growing up, I had all of this built up anger and resentment towards him and in my mind, I would unleash it all on him one day so he could feel my pain. That day never came.

It had been a long time since I'd seen him. He was lying in a hospital bed, unconscious. I'd been there for a long time, waiting for him to open his eyes and see me. I thought that maybe his illness would be the window of opportunity for us to have a real conversation about my feelings. But as his daughter, I at least wanted to be sure he was okay. When he opened his eyes for the first time in days, I greeted him and started making small talk. He didn't recognize me at all and insisted that I leave.

I didn't see him again until years later at my brother's wedding. I came into the church and my father's face lit up. He yelled out to me. "Bernadette! How you been?" He mistook me for my mother. The massive stroke that hospitalized him the last time we saw each other had resulted in major memory loss. My father still didn't know who I was. All of my life he has been a stranger to me. Now I was the same to him. As embarrassed and disappointed as I was, I still wanted to know this man, to try to make things right between us somehow or at least do my part. God gave me a glimmer of hope.

I took a seat in the sanctuary and my father came and sat down beside me. He placed his arm around my shoulder and we sat just like that. In the midst of the ceremony, he turned to me. "Hey Tokeitha, I know who are. Man, I'm so proud of you." My floodgate of tears opened and I sobbed in his arms. God gave us both what we needed—peace. My father had a moment of clarity. I had a moment as his daughter. I came that day with all of these hurtful words on my heart and my tongue, but God wasn't having it. I released all of my pain at that wedding and headed to the reception as if a load had been lifted off of me. My father and I spent the evening together, and it was as if we had never had lost time. He apologized so many times that day. He told me that he wanted to do better and to be involved in my son's life. I'm thankful God gave me an opportunity to make amends. Some people aren't lucky enough to get that chance.

Have you forgiven your father for his wrongdoing? What will it take to be forgiven?

____

____

____

____

Describe how being fatherless has affected you?

____

____

____

____

If you had one opportunity to see your father, what would you tell him? Write your response below and read it aloud.

____

____

____

I am so thankful that I have been blessed to have broken the cycle of fatherless children with my son. His father and I have moved on with our lives, but we have learned to work together for the best interest of our son. Was it easy? Not at all. But it's possible. It takes work. It takes two people willing to sacrifice everything for their child. And in our case, it took our son expressing his feelings to us to force us to realize how our differences were hurting him.

My little guy would talk to us one-on-one and have deep conversations about what he would see and ask why. I've always encouraged him to express himself to me and share his heart. We call it pillow talk. When he says, "Mom, I want to talk," I stop whatever I'm doing and give him my undivided attention because I know what that means. He is in his flow. My son lays back and lets it all out. It's normally at night before bedtime, and sometimes he's playing me to stay up late but I allow him that time. After a few pillow talks about the issues between me and his dad, we decided to set our issues aside and put our son first. Sadly it took a child to make two adults act right. Although we are not together and have fought the toughest fights, we both LOVE our son. We created a king, thus his name.

My son and his father have a bond that's so beautiful. He and his father spend time together and do some of the craziest things. There are times he does not support my son financially, and while being the sole provider for Messiah is a heavy burden to bear, I've made my peace with it. His support comes in the form of fathering his son. Resources will come, but I can't replace his father. My son can pick up the phone to call his father whenever he needs to. They spend time together. He feels safe and confident because of it. So having to forgive his father for hurting me is worth the cost of forgiveness and the peace I've granted my son. It's not a decision or a situation that can work for everyone, but it works for us. We all WIN.

For my mothers who are battling fathers over child support or visitation and it's tearing your family apart, what about the children? It's so easy for us to get caught up in our feelings, issues, and needs, but we have to stop and think about how our children are being affected. Black children are suffering dearly without their fathers. There are so many fathers already absent from their lives due to incarceration and we increase those numbers when we keep fathers out of our children's lives for other reasons that have nothing to do with them. Mother to mother, don't punish your son or daughter. Remember our children didn't ask to be here—that was a decision we made as parents.

Let's continue to break this cycle. If the father is available and willing, allow him to be there. Your child is too precious to be fatherless.

I would have loved to have had my father growing up, but I rose anyway. No, a fatherless home is not ideal, but can, and do, survive and thrive. I fought and sacrificed for my son to have his father in his life because that wasn't what happened for me. And I share my experience so that women can hear both sides of the story and, hopefully, choose differently. I've lived the good, bad, and the ugly of parenting but I am glad I didn't wallow in it. A few years ago, Pam, who I call my fairy godmother, gave me a piece of advice that I never forgot.

Grow up.

Short, sweet, and profound. You see, when we have to put our feelings aside to make the best decisions for our children, we have to grow up. Ladies, we have to push past hurt, and make amends with our own fathers so that we can have peace. To make it through the fire of life, we have to grow up.

When we have to raise these children to be strong, brave, and brilliant, we have to grow up.

The bible says in Psalm 68:5, "God is a father to the fatherless." Jeremiah 1:5 says, "I knew you before I formed you in your mother's womb." These two scriptures remind us that God knew what He was doing when he created the world and those in it. When we need a father, He is there. He created us all to be just like that phoenix—bold and resilient. We have come through the fire, through the ashes, and will have no choice but to continue to rise. Trust in your Father. We are too precious to be fatherless.

Too *Precious* to be…

Negative

There is an army of
Haters
Critics
Skeptics
Backstabbers
Perpetrators
Dreamkillers
All waiting for you to fail
THRIVE!

I took algebra in school, and in class I started to learn about patterns and repetition. As a student in the Health and Human Services program at Eastern Senior High School and as a science major in college, algebra is where it all begins. Fundamentally, algebra is about positive and negative values and finding the step-by-step solution. I can recall trying to figure out how to start a problem with broken pieces and to fit them together to get an answer.

Negativity is very similar to algebra. It's not just a single step. A negative attitude is the result, but the roots can be feelings like anger, insecurity, jealousy, rage, loneliness, and hate. Then add loss, like the death of a child, spouse, or relative. Add more bad news of a chronic illness or an unexpected diagnosis that requires medical attention.

Your life can become a whirlwind of issues while the solutions evade you like a difficult math problem.

What are the negative things going on in your life?

____

____

____

____

Where is the greatest amount of negativity in your life?

____

____

____

____

If you remove the negative, what positives will increase? (health, finances, mental state, etc.)

____

____

____

For three years, I lived in a negative world. I created most of it, adding drama, chaos, and confusion to my life by feeding the victimhood, despair, and defeat I had gathered from years of abuse. Phrases like, “I can’t” and “I don’t care” were the norm for me. Everything about me was defeated. Then I would play the blame game. I would go down the list and attach a person to a problem. My anger was my father’s fault for not being in my life. My heartache was from my toxic relationships, and my bitterness was from my childhood. I had an excuse for it all. My pain was everyone’s fault but my own.

When you’re speaking negativity into the atmosphere, do you ever feel drained afterwards? That’s because words are powerful.

Negative energy comes through people as well. Think about who we surround ourselves with in our personal, professional, or spiritual life. I used to work on an all-female team. We were an emotionally charged group of vocal, opinionated women. Everyone in the office would watch us like hawks. They always wanted to see if we work together as a team the way we appeared on the outside, poised and polished. Honestly, behind closed doors, we argued and took hours to agree even on the smallest things. We all knew why. There was one woman in the group, who always wanted to go left when we went right. Here’s the lesson: Everyone doesn’t belong in your space. Sometimes one person can make the entire group toxic.

We counteracted that negativity with preparation. We knew what to expect and we always had a solution to whatever issue our teammate would bring up. That was one effective way to counteract the negativity. Having a choice can make or break a situation easily.

When you're in a negative state of mind, what are some of the choices you make or have made?

____

____

____

____

Do you find that when you act out on your negative emotions, you devalue yourself? Why?

____

____

____

____

Has your negativity caused you to have any of the following?

- □ Stress
- □ Bitterness
- □ Anxiety
- □ Depression
- □ Resentment
- □ Guilt

I can raise my hand in the air for each one. But here's the thing that's so interesting. Before I could sort through my emotions, I attributed all of these feelings to someone or something else. I didn't realize I had the power to change. I didn't realize I didn't have to claim any of these feelings if I didn't want to. I lost so much time wallowing in my despair. God, I would give anything to have that time and energy back.

But once that shift occurred for me, I was like fire! When I was unhappy on my government job, I found a new one. I didn't sit there year after year complaining about how poor management was and how I couldn't get a promotion. I took control. Now I love what I do and I do what I love. It's nothing like waking up happy every day. I'm not miserable during my morning commute or in bad weather because this is the life I chose, not someone else. I am not drained by toxic work environments and people.

If you are, release that negativity from your life. Find a career you love and make a decision today to make it happen.

Do you work in a toxic work environment?

____

____

____

____

How has the toxic work environment affected your productivity?

____

____

____

What can you do to make a difference on the job?

____

____

____

____

A bit more about work. Too much negativity can lead to stress and you don't need it. Don't allow the negative people at work to obstruct or hinder your productivity. Be mindful of those people who want to stand at your desk and rant all day or those venting sessions that contaminate the entire office. Avoid the daily dish of gossip and office politics which is a wildfire waiting to spread. Before you know it you will be engulfed in flames and consumed by the rumors and scandals.

Now let's get into those personal relationships. Remember you have a choice about who you allow into your life. Friends and family can be just as draining as coworkers, and sometimes even more. They are in our personal space and we have emotional ties to them. So we can't fire them like we would our boss or wipe the board clean as we would to start over a math problem. But that doesn't mean you're stuck, either. Decide what relationships are good for you, keep those, and make the move to let the others go. It won't be cut and dry, but in the end, you'll feel so much better without that negative weight on you.

Do you have a friend who has been calling you in tears for years over her dysfunctional relationship? Put her at the top of the list. We all have that negative home girl whose opinion is always negative. She is constantly putting others down. No matter the circumstances, nothing is ever right, whether it's the food, the environment, or the people. Everything is wrong. If a person finds something wrong with everything, all the time, then move on. The gossip, the complaining, the bad mood—who needs it? Not you. You don't want to be that friend that everyone avoids. But that's exactly who you'll be if you don't cut this one loose.

It's amazing how change occurs the moment the negativity is removed from our lives. It's a lesson I've personally lived. The moment I let go, my finances were free. My finances were no longer cursed. He may have left the bills behind, but I had more money to invest into me and my child instead of a man. My life turned around because I ushered in the positive and waved goodbye to the negative. Believe me, it works.

If you think the church is negativity-free, think again. Even in the place where God commanded us to LOVE all, there is hypocrisy from the pulpit to the back row of pews. I go to church and have seen negativity up close and personal. It's not shocking to me. You get just as many side-eyes, and just as much judgement and rude behavior in the church as you do outside. Sad but true. You can't escape it. But you can control how you respond to it.

Do you find yourself surrounded with negative people at church?

____

____

____

What positive steps will you take to remove the negativity from your spiritual life? For example: prayer changes things, so praying may be your option.

____

____

____

____

____

Understand that you can absorb the same negative energy at church that you can at work or anywhere else. Like an algebra problem, you have to find another solution. Remember when you keep multiplying a zero you get a zero, so come up with a better way. I have had my share of pain, disappointment, and discouragement. Negativity has threaten to take over my life. But for every negative, there was a positive. I want you to find those positive paths so you can live a fuller, happier, and healthier life. Let the haters hate and those who want (not have to) to wallow in wasted time do that.
You, Queen, have work to do.

You are too precious to be negative.

Too *Precious* to be...

Ungrateful

Giving is your best form of currency.

We use instruments to measure many things. A sphygmometer is used to measure blood pressure. To measure our weight we would use a scale. Rulers, tape measures, yardsticks, and odometers measure length and protractors measure angles. We can measure just about anything.

Are there any devices to measure gratitude? Can we measure an act of kindness or a thank you? If we were to assess ourselves when it comes to gratefulness and appreciation, where would we stand?

Showing gratitude takes discipline. Graciousness is a muscle, and we have to use it regularly if we expect it be strong. Like an athlete exercises and conditions, we need to do the same with giving thanks.

So how do we do it?

Say "Thank You."

Give away something for free.

Surprise someone with a kind gesture.

Give a hug.

Have an acknowledgement ritual, such as prayer or meditation.

These are just a few examples, but there are so many more. This is a list of small acts of kindness, but each has a big impact.

Giving verbal thanks is one of the easiest things to do, but it's often done the least. We have the opportunity to say, "Thank you" or "I appreciate you" at least ten times a day. Whenever someone hands you something, holds the door for you, compliments you on your shoes, thank them. When you open your eyes in the morning, thank God for another day. If you are out of practice, the more you do it, I promise the easier it will become.

Being grateful is not always about receiving; it's about giving, too. When you can be a blessing to someone, do it. Buy lunch or coffee for your co-worker, treat a friend to a manicure, or maybe if you sell books or products, give a customer or a local person in need a gift for free. If it costs you time or a little money, it's okay. Sow a seed!

Surprises really bring out a person's true emotions, and for most of us they are heartwarming. I've always loved them and so does my mother. I earned it honestly. My mom is the best at surprises; she can hold it until that perfect moment. My mom would always listen to me and my daddy talk about our wishes and things we wanted, take note, and then make them happen for us. I promised I would create that same fun environment for my son with surprises he loves, so I do it as often as I can.

Isn't it an awesome feeling to receive a gift? Any gift is wonderful, but a free gift is really something special. I've been blessed with so many gifts, and each one has made such a difference in my life. Sometimes, the impact has been small and other times, it's been major. The Bartko Foundation, a nonprofit that supports single mothers, helped me to become a homeowner. After my home was robbed a few Christmases ago, my family and friends replaced all of the presents that were stolen.

That was a rough time, but I was so grateful that my son and I were safe and that our support circle rallied around us with support. I was humbled by the outpouring of love we received and that far outweighed the anger I felt about my home being violated. Just another reminder to focus more on the beauty of the rainbow than the storm that came before it. There is always something to be grateful for in every situation. Our situation could have been worse. The outcome could have been different. But I wasn't going to block our continuous flow of blessings with ungratefulness. Not only would that have been disrespectful to our family, it would have been disrespectful to God.

Let's think about all that a hug can do. A warm embrace can be an exchange of positive energy and convey an instant sense of gratitude. A hug can lift someone's spirits and bring a smile to their face. A hug can provide feelings of security. Have you ever thought about if we could hug the entire world, how much happier we all could be?

Prayer is how we give thanks to God, and open our hearts to gratitude. In the morning, I start my day thanking God. I give Him thanks before my feet hit the floor. I say, "Thank you GOD for allowing me to see another day." I listen to something inspirational (usually Dr. Cindy Trimm's Atomic Prayer, Warfare Prayer, or worship music) to create a peaceful atmosphere and invite God into my space.

I begin my prayer asking for clarity and for God to remove any interference, hindrance, or barriers. I ask for godly council, healing, restoration, and strength. I get more specific and petition on the behalf of family and friends and those who are on my heart such as my son, family, businesses, health, finances, and place of employment. I pray for covering and protection throughout the day. I pray for those attached to me spiritually such as my pastor, first lady, and partners of my church. Whatever is on my heart, I take it to God in prayer.

Here's an example of my morning prayer:

Heavenly Father in the name of Jesus Christ, I welcome you right now into my mind, body, and soul. Remove all fear, malice, disobedience, and wickedness from my mind, body, and soul. Holy Spirit, set this atmosphere right now, increase in me, and syncopate me with the heavens. I ask, in Jesus' name, that you would align me with the heavens and that I am in right standing with you. Remove the weight and release the pressure as I cast my cares unto you. Father, I give your name praise for without you I am nothing. I ask that my angel and the legions of angels you appointed to me go to work on my behalf right now. In the name of Jesus, I ask that every cell, tissue, organ, and system within my body be injected with forgiveness and love. Father I ask with a humble heart that you give me energy to endure, determination to win, and the will to live as I walk this spiritual walk with you. I speak life over my family, household, business, finances, health, place of employment, and my community. May my hands be prosperous to your kingdom as I serve your people. As a child of the most high GOD, I thank you that you didn't leave me in the state in condition that I once was in but that you brought me up and out of the fire. Forgive those who I have hurt and who have hurt me intentionally or unintentionally, knowingly or unknowingly. Father I ask that you protect and insulate me, my son, and those attached to my bloodline on both sides that no hurt, harm, or danger will come upon us in anyway. I send notice to Satan, his army, and any one acting in the form of a satanic or demonic attack that they have no power, authority, or ability to penetrate me, my son, or those attached to me on both sides of my bloodline. No weapon formed against us shall prosper. Break, loose, and free me from every chain of bondage. I come against and pull down every ungodly soul tie, generational curse, word curse, and all calamities in and around me, my son, and those attached to me on both sides of my bloodline. Break and loose every chain in my community that it is free from poverty, abuse, drugs, prostitution, violence, alcohol and any other inference of this world in Jesus' name.

When I pray for my church, I add details:

I pray that my pastor, first lady, and partners of New Life Christian Center Church are covered by the blood of Jesus Christ so that nothing will be missing, broken, or lacking in their lives. Restore and replenish the Man of God at New Life Christian Center Church with all that is needed to preach and teach your word. Fill his cup so that the ministry will not be a burden. Allow our congregation to be 100% tithers and provide us with multiple streams of income so that you get the glory, honor, and praise you deserve. Send the resources and increase from the north, south, east, and west, by land, sea, and air to the ministry of New Life Christian Center Church and the kingdom of GOD some triple fold.

When I pray for this nation, our President, and my family members in various branches of government:

Cover this nation, region, state, county, city, and my community with resources, peace, and stability. In GOD we trust, I pray for President Obama, legislators, and public offi-

cials that our leaders are receiving godly council and are wise in their decisions. Father I ask that you protect those in authoritative positions over our lives. Protect our leaders as they travel abroad. Be a shield for those who risk their lives for our county, leaders, and the government. I lift up to you our family members that serve and protect the government. May they receive the proper healing and a super natural blessing of abundance for their sacrifice. I pray for peace and understanding, let your light shine and every Jericho wall come down in Jesus name.

Those are just a few examples of what and how I may pray when I start my day. I pray whenever, wherever. My day can start as early as 5:00 a.m. and end as late as @CEOAzarel on Twitter after dark. Regardless, I make sure prayer is a priority. There is no limit to the amount of time I pray nor is there a limit to the time of day.

Somebody prayed for me, and one thing I know for sure is that prayer works! There is power in prayer. My grandmother prayed for my mother, my mother prays for me and my sister, and I pray for my son as well. All of those prayers add up! I condition myself to pray just like Floyd Mayweather trains for a championship fight. Every day I have to work my muscles, and that includes exercising, giving thanks with strategic prayers, and praying for specific situations in and around me. I pray whenever and around whomever, especially if I feel something isn't right. To be honest, I have even prayed while I was committing sin. I have prayed in the club, under the influence of alcohol, before, during, and after intercourse. If I was in trouble, I prayed. If I needed God, I prayed. We all have had those moments. "Please Lord, if you get me out of this one, I promise..."

"Oh GOD can you let me make it home safe."

"I know this is wrong, but GOD please help me out this mess."

Am I telling the truth? I know the saints act like they don't do any wrong. Well let me be the first to say that I have been wrong, ignorant, and stupid at times. But like the lyrics to the song remind us, "He thought I was worth saving." I'm worth it and God gets the glory regardless. He has a way of getting what He wants.

I didn't grow up in a religious household, but I always saw the women in my home praying. I never forgot that.

Giving thanks isn't easy for everyone. Sometimes we have to condition ourselves to be more grateful. We have to condition our hearts to release bitterness and to be positive not negative. It can be easier said than done, right?

One of the biggest lessons was learning to be grateful even when things didn't go my way. Yes, I have goals and ambitions. I have desires of my heart and wants and needs. Yet even when God delays my blessings or doesn't answer my prayers in my time, I had to realize that I could still give praise for what I already had. It took me some time to get to that heart space. Whew! I would get frustrated, disappointed, and hurt. A lemon had nothing on me. I was so bitter. And it stemmed from my challenge with letting go. When I wanted something, I wanted it. But I grew up! (Even as an adult.) I started to condition my mind and body to acknowledge gratitude and I saw my happiness rise.

I was too precious to be ungrateful.

Children are such a beautiful reminder to stay grateful. My son has loved vacuum cleaners since he was one years old. While other kids ask for the latest gaming system, my son wants a vacuum for any occasion. Today, we have 3. He has had ever brand except a Dyson. Although I can't afford a Dyson yet, I know one day I will. When I do he is going to be ecstatic. Whenever I purchase the latest model for him, he says to me, "Mommy, you're the best." When I hear those words, I know that's Grade A satisfaction. My little guy is so thankful for some of simplest things in life. He teaches me more than he will ever know. He is too precious to be ungrateful.

What person in your life has shown you the most gratitude?

____

____

____

____

What life-altering event caused you to be grateful? If so, explain how you became thankful.

____

____

____

____

Being ungrateful puts a limit on your happiness.

Are you ungrateful?

____

____

____

____

Are you always complaining even when there's nothing wrong?

____

____

____

____

Do you start your day by giving thanks? Why or Why not?

____

____

____

____

I can say thank you for so many things. For example, I'm thankful for being in my right state of mind. I'm thankful that I'm in good health and free from disease. I am grateful that all of my limbs, organs, and systems are fully functional. I'm thankful that my son is healthy and that he has the liberty to climb, play, run, and jump every day. I'm thankful for the roof over our head, clothes on our back, food on the table, and our mode of transportation. I'm thankful for our appliances and that every season they are operating to the fullest capacity without malfunction. I'm thankful for love and support from my various families whether it is my bloodline, social media, church, workplace family. I'm thankful for the ability to travel and visit love ones. I'm thankful for those who support me, invest in me, or make a difference in my life. I'm thankful for peace, stability, love, endurance, wisdom, knowledge, and resilience.

I am most thankful for my Boo—and that's God. (Yes, I say that.) He is my Higher Power, and I found that when I give him all my love and treat him like the man He is in my life, He shows up and shows out. No one can out do my Boo. There is no instrument on earth that can measure him. I can care less what people will say about how I address Him. But I will say this; He has been the best thing that has happened to me. I'm too precious to be ungrateful.

List 10 things you're grateful for…

I am grateful for ____________________________________

I am grateful for ____________________________________

I am grateful for ____________________________________

I am grateful for____________________________________

I am grateful for____________________________________

I am grateful for____________________________________

I am grateful for____________________________________

I am grateful for____________________________________

I am grateful for____________________________________

I am grateful for____________________________________

When you look at your 10 items, did you gain or achieve any of them alone? For example, I'm grateful for my son, but I didn't make him by myself. List those, too.

____

____

____

Explain how you did it all alone.

____

____

____

____

List an accomplishment you have achieved on your own.

____

____

____

____

I've found that these steps helped me to become more grateful:

Reading scriptures or affirmations

Being flexible and adapting

Eliminating low self-esteem and self-pity

For me reading the Bible has help along with other inspirational books. I really like to screenshot affirmations from social media and repeat them to myself. I also write them down on small pieces of paper and I'll find them at a later time. Sometimes it's the right time, just like you would open a fortune cookie. Affirmations can give you a burst of confidence. Do you know that there is power in your tongue? Do you speak life into every dead, negative, or dark situation? Here are a few examples of affirmations that you may find to be helpful.

I see endless opportunities before me. (This is one of my favorites.)

I am beautiful.

I am worth loving.

I am worthy of love and respect.

No one can take care of me more than I can.

I am a conquer.

I cannot learn other people's lessons for them.

I am in control of my destiny.

I am perfect exactly as I am.

I accept myself although I may make mistakes.

Always a lesson, never a failure.

My hands are prosperous.

I am divinely protected.

I am open to receive.

I owe no explanations.

I heal quickly and easily.

I can be changed by what happens to me. But I refuse to be reduced by it-Maya Angelou

"Success in life comes when you simply refuse to give up, when you have goals so strong that obstacles, failure & loss only act as motivation" Russell Simmons

I love when affirmations come in the form of a text

message. My friends and I share them often. It doesn't mean we are going through anything; it's one of those just-because moments. Again those moments can be just as profound. We have so much to be grateful for and life is too precious to be ungrateful. Make a list, repeat your daily affirmations, and speak life into every component: physically, mentally, financially, emotionally, and spiritually.

Every day I say to myself, "I must condition myself to be GREAT." One may ask how do you condition yourself to be great. There are ways to condition yourself to be thankful and grateful for all things big or small. Start today by taking small steps:

Dedicate time to pray, worship, meditate every day.

Exercise love and forgiveness by practicing, patience and honesty, with an open heart.

Become a giver and develop a mindset to serve others.

We all have so much to be thankful for in life.

You are too precious to be ungrateful.

Too *Precious* to be...

Inferior

You don't need permission to be great.
You just need an opportunity.

"Too precious to be...What have you overcome? Fill in the blank with words from your journey."
I posted this on my Instagram page recently, and as I read through the responses one in particular caught my eye. *Inferior, fearful, and unchallenged.* It was from Jada Thornton, one of my followers. *Inferior.* I was so touched by Jada's response that I had to speak to it in this book. (Thank you, Jada, for your openness and inspiration.) She is not alone.

When a woman feels inferior in any capacity, the reason is simple. She does not know her position or her power.

Interestingly, another Jada—Jada Pinkett-Smith, wife of actor Will Smith—posted something to her Facebook page a few years ago about her role in her husband's life. It was so profound to me that I saved it and I refer to it often. She shared "three steps behind [her king] is the most powerful position for a Queen. Anything that comes toward him from behind, I encounter first. I can clearly see what advances to his right and his left. I also have my sights on what approaches ahead." Yes, Jada!

After reading this post, it affirmed for me just how powerful women are. I thought about how often women smile and strategically move or strike when needed, just like a queen on a chess board. Women have so much power to rule, replace, and conquer. It is our birthright. We simply need to walk in it.

We are too precious to be inferior.

Despite who we are and how we should be treated in the world, in some countries (including the United States) we are treated as less than by one another and from the opposite sex. It's in a women's nature to be loving and gentle. But it is important that we do not allow anyone to take our kindness for a weakness. My kindness is a weapon, and if you're not careful, you may find yourself defenseless against this Queen.

Who are the Queens in your life? List the women of power within your network. You will see just how much power is at your fingertips. Your network can be within your family, in church, your gym, workplace, college roommates, leaders, or social media groups.

____

____

____

____

____

Powerful women like Venus and Serena Williams and Ronda Rousey show us strength in their athleticism. Michelle Obama, Oprah Winfrey, Misty Copeland, and Hillary Clinton are incredible women in service, business, performing art, and politics. They lead by example and show us that women don't need to be inferior. That includes our sisters abroad who face more belittling circumstances that anyone could imagine.

Just like a queen in chess, a woman should be mobile and free. But that is not the reality for some women who are ostracized from acid attacks. An acid attack is when someone intentionally throws a chemical on a woman's face, head, or body to disfigure her. As a result of an attack, women are left blind, disabled, or maimed. Strong acids such as nitric and sulfuric acids leave scars and permanent disfigurement. Some women commit suicide as a result of being attacked and many of these incidents go unreported. These horrific violations occur for any number of reasons, from a dispute to revenge.

This senseless violence impacts women around the world and it has to be stopped.

What harm or act of violence has someone done to you or a woman in your family?

____

____

____

____

Do you resent the person? Describe your feelings because you were treated as an inferior.

____

____

____

____

What can you do to mend the brokenness?

____

____

____

____

Without secretly wishing harm on someone, how can you forgive?

____

____

____

____

If you or someone you know has been a victim of an acid attack, visit www.acidviolence.org

A woman's body is her identity from the day she is born. We are constantly being judged and evaluated based on how we look. We sacrifice so much just to be accepted and fit in. From straightening or curling our hair, covering our bodies to keep men from being tempted, or binding ourselves in undergarments that confine us to shape and mold us into whatever we think the world wants to see or to feel good. Oh but to be free!

With a voice and knowledge we are an endangered species, hunted by the world.

Do undergarments like body shapers and slimmers make you feel inferior? Describe your feelings.

____

____

____

____

Do you feel that these undergarments make you conform to society image of women? Explain your answer.

____

____

____

____

I was fortunate to have a daddy that treated me like a queen. He taught me to respect my body and to always dress appropriately. He always made sure I was well-rounded. He taught me everything about football and boxing. He also taught me how to shoot so I would always know how to protect myself in case he can't come to my rescue. I want that for as many girls as possible. We have to encourage our girls to have relationships with their father. A father is the first king a girl encounters; from him, she should learn what a queen is supposed to be.

It's not always pretty being a queen. A queen's work is never done. She can endure the hardest of tasks and still move. You are that queen.You are meant to be protected. You are that powerful. You are like that lioness using precision to develop your skills. Continue to show the world how powerful you are through your smile, the click of your heels, or the twinkle in your eye. Show the world your power from the pulpit, the boardroom, and the bedroom.

You are too precious to be inferior.

Too *Precious* to be...

Disrespected

If manipulation is your best feature, please diversify your portfolio.

Reptiles have some of the toughest skin known to the animal kingdom. Their dry, scaly coating acts a shield—protecting these cold-blooded creatures from the sun and heat. Skin, for a reptile, is like armor. As humans, we develop armor, too. When we are repeatedly hurt, abused, or attacked, we become angry, defensive, and protective. When someone threatens to harm us, our initial response is to fight back and defend ourselves. Sometimes, our innate responses are warranted; other times not.

If you are coming to disrespect me, I bite first and ask questions later.

I am too precious to be disrespected.

Being disrespected by someone can really test your tolerance, patience, and your thought process. We have all been taught to "ignore" or "turn the other cheek." It's true; not all battles can or should be fought. It's always good to do what is morally right. Choose good over evil. God wants us to take the high road at all times. But there are those times when you have to react. You have to defend yourself. You are too precious to be disrespected.

I've had more than my share of disrespect. I don't believe that a lack of respect is an accident. People who disrespect you know it. They are speaking badly about you to someone else, making jokes to your face, dismissing your point-of-view, and we can't forget the infamous Instagram and Twitter rants that go viral. How many times have you heard the excuse, "I don't mean any harm"? That lame statement does not erase bad behavior. Period.

We all know what disrespect looks, feels, and sounds like. So for someone to say they didn't mean to be hurtful towards you is simply untrue.

We all have our list of things that we consider to be highly disrespectful and some actions rank higher than others. For me, spitting on someone is number one. It has happened to me before, and in front of my son. I was in the midst of an argument with the person, and as his car pulled off, their foul spit landed on the sleeve of my jacket. I should have lost my mind but I would have lost my child. Instead of snapping I drove to the nearest police station. I ended up settling the situation in court, and I had the jacket as evidence to show to the judge months later. Unbelievable! God fought that battle for me, and I won my case. Won't He do it!

I've had liquor thrown in my face; I've been cursed at, and hit. There have been countless times where I thought I have been pushed beyond my limits. I've sang right along with DMX, "Y'all goin' make me lose my mind, UP in here!

UP in here!" God has only given me what I can bear. I'm grateful to be alive and able to write about my life's journey. I am too precious to be disrespected. You are too precious to be disrespected.

Who do you allow to penetrate or manipulate your emotions?

____

____

____

____

How have you reacted to be being disrespected?

____

____

____

____

How do you keep from snapping or losing self-control?

____

____

____

____

Do you take the time to reflect on the outcomes of the disrespect?

Hate is like that cancerous tumor full of malice. It should be removed. Hate is very strong; to hate someone means you have no remorse or guilt for what you do. To hate someone shows no kindness, mercy, or gentleness. You are just like that cold-blooded reptile. I encountered hate multiple times as a college student at a Southern college. Bennett College is historically known for racial incidents, including the Greensboro Massacre and the Greensboro Sit-in, dating back to the Civil Rights Movement. Sadly, racism was still an issue for me and other students years later.

I was at the local bookstore searching for a biology book for a class. I headed back to my car and there was a young couple parked next to me. A young lady was driving and she struggled to back out of the space. With their window rolled down, I could hear the man with her shouting at her, "Back out the car!" She starts to panic. "Back the car up, it's just a fucking nigger!" He repeated it over and over again, as the lady tapped my car repeatedly to maneuver out of the lot. Enraged, I put my purple Chevy Caprice in reverse, switched the gear to drive, and mashed on the gas chasing them down the street. I whizzed through the streets as if I were a police cruiser chasing a suspect on the run. Within minutes, I'd reported the incident. The police had a full description of the young couple, the tag number of the car, and proof on my scratched car. The police found them and I pressed every charge possible.

I was too precious to be disrespected.

It hurts me when I see any women disrespected, especially our girls. I've witnessed young women being physically and verbally assaulted, and it's heartbreaking. It makes me think of how many times I could have lost my cool and made a bad decision that could have cost me my job, my child, or my life. I had to develop a tough skin so I could learn not to always react with my mouth or hands first, but with my mind instead. We have a responsibility to teach our young people to do the same. That mindset requires discipline and gratitude—I know I have too much to lose. They do, too.

What can you do to help the next generation understand just how tough life can be?

____

____

____

____

I challenge you to choose one young person or one youth organization to help stop that cycle of disrespect. Our children are too precious to be disrespected.

Respect yourself enough to help someone else.

Too *Precious* to be... *Deceived*

Someone has to witness your level of success to succeed.

The good thing about being a mom to a young man is that I get to play with his toys. My favorite is his Transformers set. He has the entire fleet. I love Optimus Prime and my favorite guy is Bumble Bee. Go Bee! I love Bumble Bee because he is edgy. Not only do we have a collection at home, but we also watch all of the movies. My son is all about the action. I come for that, too, but the eye candy doesn't hurt either (I'm just saying, a girl has to give credit where it's due.) But when we think about it, Transformers offer so many lessons for women. The Number One Transformer Teaching? Deception.

Optimus Prime is the Transformer's fearless leader. Nothing gets past him, especially a Decepticon. An Autobot appears fresh, sleek, fast, and luxurious. What's not to love? Those Decepticons are no good. That shiny exterior doesn't fool Optimus or his team. And we see that same fraud in our day to day lives.

People appear helpful, innocent, honest, and kind on

the outside. But how many times in life have we been fooled? We may think that we have a friend who is sincere and trustworthy, when in reality they are an imposter. Just like the Decepticons, they look like they belong; they talk like they belong, but they're full of lies and betrayal. We need to look at people from a microscopic view, not just on the surface. You are too precious to be deceived.

So how do you know if you're being deceived? Just like in the culinary world, presentation is everything. People present themselves in many forms from shy to outspoken, private to open, and the list goes on. Think about all of those people in and around you and how they act. What type of actions are displayed? Are they a fraud? They may possess any of the following character flaws:

Difficult
Arrogant
Irrational
Selfish
Manipulative
Insensitive
Heartless
Cunning
Evil
Conniving
Wicked
Stingy
Rude
Scheming

Have you been betrayed by a friend? Male or female? Explain how?

____

____

____

____

We always have to remember that we are human and being hurt is part of the experience. None of us want it, but it will happen. The key is to avoid the hurt that we can see coming from miles ahead.

Sometimes as women, we let our defenses down when we get comfortable and begin to trust someone. We get lured in by the deceit. As people we can be blinded by the facade. Behind all the makeup or cologne, is there anything real?

If we sense fraud, we have to listen to our inner voice. Use your discernment and get out fast! Everyone we encounter doesn't have a good heart, even when they seem sweet and pure. Looks can be deceiving; you could be in the presence of a devil in a blue dress or suit.

Take the time to get to know them. That one step can save you so much heartache.

How should you handle a deceiving person? It's as easy as 1-2-3.
Unmask the truth
Keep your guards up
Don't allow them to get under your skin

What area in your life have you been deceived?

____

Deception is so rampant in business. In business relationships, you should never feel as if you're one-sided or off balance when working with a partner. Both sides should bring equal parts to the table. Listen with open ears to what is being said. I received some of the best advice from a friend once. He warned me to be careful who I shared my dreams with. (Thank you Jap!) I gave it some thought and I totally understand that some individuals don't want you to surpass them.

Now I am passing those same pearls of wisdom on to you. Everyone isn't trustworthy; protect your thoughts and dreams. It's ironic that people can say, "Congratulations" or "I'm so happy for you" when you are working towards your goals. But how many people will really show up and invest? I started a Kickstarter campaign for this book. I needed assistance in covering the publishing costs. My campaign ran for 45 days and I never met the goal. All of the people who said they would support me, they all disappeared. I sent text messages, emails, posters, and did everything else I could. Yet these are the same people who will send a first-class invitation to their baby shower, bridal shower, birthday party, and housewarming.

Be leery of those who take from you but don't give.

Name a time and situation when people promised to support you.

____

____

____

Name an instance when you received little to no support from those close to you.

____

____

____

____

As an author I often chat with fellow writers. My sister and friend of @BellaBee books, Maisha, gave me some great advice one night during one of our discussions. She said we have to lead by example, at times take the high road, and to remember we can't control others. That's what happens when we transform as women. We don't lose ourselves along the way. We enhance ourselves.

There are many people who may support you openly but behind closed doors they want to see you fail, because you were creative or have an amazing idea. Everyone doesn't celebrate your accomplishments on the road to success.

It's natural for you to lose friends as you climb. Don't take it personal. There are always people in the world that are not original and will copy because there are not authentic. No one can clone you.

You have to protect yourself. Stay alert. Anything or anyone can be a diversion and keep you from achieving your goals or following your dreams. A diversion can be a distraction, hindrance, barrier, or barricade in the form of a relationship, liaison, associate, business partner, or colleague. Beware!

Who and What are the distractions in your life?

____

____

____

____

How do you plan to remove the distraction? What will you do differently?

____

____

____

____

You don't have time to waste with distractions. Remember you are unstoppable. Practice self-control at all times, like Optimus Prime. He keeps his cool because he knows he is the leader and everyone counts on him to be just that. The people around you know that you're a threat and they will try every attack possible to take you out. You are that precious!

You're so powerful that evil will always be present. Your greatness is a threat. Don't ignore those deception signs. Everyone has a job and some people are fabricated to use and abuse.

You are valuable.
You are loved.
Every dream inside of you is worth fighting for.

You are too precious to be anything or anyone but YOU.

Conclusion...

I had an ugly start in life, but it didn't break me. My ugly start was just the beginning. God created me to be a force to benefit others and change the world. **I am too precious to be broken or dimmed.**

I'm a butterfly; I don't look like what I have been through. I didn't know it in the fire, but all of my pain and disappointment transformed me. I needed each and every one of those life lessons to carry with me. **I am too precious not to fly.**

I learned that life is a requirement and death is NOT an option. I choose life. **I am too precious to be dead.**

I've learned how to forgive, starting with myself. **I am too precious to be bitter.**

This book is the launch of my God-given purpose. He is weaving everything I've ever done—all of the people, the experiences, the lessons—together and laying the path to my assignment. I am here to support you and women around the world to grow their faith, realize their potential, and live the lives that God has created for them. He has called me to empower women to rise up and to be trailblazers. What has He called you to do?

I want you to know that you are an incredible woman. You are loved. You are abundantly blessed. You are prosperous. You are life. You are a queen. I want you to live without limits, to know your worth, and to step out into the world in your boldness. You are a phoenix. You are a pearl. Rare, resilient, and strong. Own and honor that. Tattoo it on your heart and your soul.

You are too precious NOT to be whatever your heart desires.

Go get it.

A Special Thank You To...

Thank you to the Potters who used their power and ability to mold me into the woman I am today: Sadie, Bernadette, Christopher, Priscilla, LaShowne, Rennie, Gloria (NY), Jackie D., Mary K., Shirley D., Tina H., Rochelle J., LaShaurn C., to my mentors Lisa S., Margaret Q., Pam O., my biggest supporters Cynthia S., Latrice S., Shelley M^{C}., Shanita L., New Life Christian Center Church, DC DHS (love to my Eckington crew), the Saddlers, my Jackson family (NC), my Bennett sisters of Bennett College especially Sharnikya Howard of Life Abundantly Coaching, John W. #3 and #4, Ty, and to all my chicas (Michelle, Brandi, Nikki) who represent over 25 years of friendship and who command, delegate, and advocate for this world.

Thank you, Curtis Watkins of RealVoices of America for my first interview. Thank you, F.L.A.M.E.S. for my first award, acknowledging Empowerment Station, LLC as an Emerging Empowerment Organization. Thank you, The Connect on BLIS.FM for my first radio interview. Thank you, Natasha T. Brown of #10Blessings10ksurvivors and my fellow Ambassadors as we work to help 10,000 victims leave abusive relationships of Domestic Violence.

Thank you to everyone who pledged their support for

the Too Precious To Be Kickstarter campaign. Thank you Janet and Monica for your time and feedback. Also a special thank you to the girl team who helped guide me in the publishing process. Thank you to Life Changing Books; CEO Tressa "Azarel" Smallwood and her assistant, Mrs. V. Greene, for all of their time and effort in the entire publishing process. I couldn't have done it without you ladies. Thank you Stephanie, Leslie, Tracy and Jamie for taking my vision to the next level. I am truly grateful for everyone.

If you feel that this book has impacted your life, please share @Empowerment Station on Facebook or tweet @TokeithaWilson, use the hash tag #TooPreciousToBe in your post. Follow me on Facebook @Empowerment Station or @TokeithaWilson on Instagram, Periscope, and Twitter. For speaking inquires visit www.empowermentstation.com

About the Author...

Behind her heart-shaped smile, Tokeitha K. Wilson is a transparent speaker. She is a true illustration of growth as she shares her experiences of humiliation, embarrassment, and failure with her audiences. Tokeitha was born and raised in the District of Columbia. She is a product of DC Public Schools. Tokeitha is a mother and lover of comedy and sports.

For More Information:

Contact Tokeitha K. Wilson at empowerment.station@gmail.com

Visit her on Instagram @tokeithawilson

Notes

Notes

Notes

Notes

www.ingramcontent.com/pod-product-compliance
Lightning Source LLC
Chambersburg PA
CBHW051839090426
42736CB00011B/1884

9780692570289